OTHER BOOKS BY

How to Book Acting Jobs in episodic and Film: Conversations with a Veteran Casting Director on Mastering the Audition Room (2009)

How to Book Acting Jobs in episodic and Film: Second Edition: The Truth About the Acting Industry—Conversations with a Veteran Casting Director (2012)

A True Hollywood Cancer Story (2018)

Little Lucky Girl: Secrets of Superman (2018)

RESPONSES TO HOW TO BOOK ACTING JOBS IN TV AND FILM: 2ND EDITION

Cathy Reinking is the real deal, and reading this book almost feels like sitting down with her & her being very generous with her time and sharing a great deal of her experience. It's not a hand-holding, "gee you're great" kind of book. It is an eye-opener and a wake-up call. As an actor in this industry you know there's a lot that is out of your control. However, there's more in your control than you may have realized, and the author discusses these things in detail. I loved the chapter on charisma. Heck, this is helpful for anyone, in any walk of life. There's info. you'll get in this book that I haven't found anywhere else. I finally understand pilot season...what it is & how it works. I now understand the difference between a multi-camera sitcom & a single-camera sitcom, and comedic films vs. episodic comedies. I've heard many times things like, "When you walk in that room, they want it to be you. They're rooting for you." I believe this is true, but after reading this book I now have a better understanding of just what that means. This will definitely be a re-read year after year.

—J. Baskette-Ridings, Actress

This book explains everything you need to know about being a professional actor in Los Angeles. It is written in very clear, concise language that imparts every detail of every aspect of this career. This is stuff you will not learn in any class, no matter how expensive or who is teaching it. There's no nebulous mumbo jumbo about "standing out" and "being different", just solid advice. The chapters on Pilot Season and Different Styles of Auditioning are worth the price several times over. Cathy pulls no punches in the Going Professional section. She discusses attitude and mindset, networking, and social media for actors, as well as advice for self-taping auditions.

This book contains the most detailed description of going to first auditions and getting called back that I've ever read.

—Denise Olson, Los Angeles Actress

How To Book Acting Jobs 3.0: Through the Eyes of a Casting Director - Across All Platforms

Cathy Reinking

DEDICATION

Kate Marie Reinking. My love for you surpasses all the love I have for actors

CONTENTS

1   Brutal Honesty   Pg 2

2   What is Good Acting?   Pg 8

3   The Different Styles of Auditioning   Pg 34

4   In-Person Auditions vs. Self-Tapes   Pg 56

5   How Do We Choose Who Gets to Audition?   Pg 80

6   Where to Live   Pg 90

7   Social Media and Being an Influencer   Pg 120

8   You are an Entrepreneur   Pg 130

9   Pilot Season   Pg 140

10   The Well-Rounded Actor   Pg 150

11   Final Words 3.0   Pg 156

    Top Ten Secrets of Charisma   Pg 162

    Blogs Reposted   Pg 166

    Duties of a Casting Director   Pg 198

    Acknowledgments   Pg 202

MY MANTRA

Acting is everything.

Acting is an art.

Actors are vessels to help us understand ourselves.

Actors are essential.

If all the actors would disappear, what would our world look like?

Actors are brave.

Actors are not afraid to reveal themselves in their darkness and their light.

What are the ways in which I can help them be their most authentic selves?

What is really important? Making a living as an actor. Otherwise you'll just be investing in a business that will never show a profit

The goal should be to quit your day job and make your money solely as an actor. In the current market place, it's getting harder and harder to do that.

My deep inside track in the business coupled with my genuine caring for the artist gives me the edge.

It's not about the red carpet or fame and fortune at all.

It's about YOU.

THE PATHS YOU TAKE

When you are a kid, teen and young adult, you have such dreams… *big* dreams… following your bliss. I wanted to be an actress so badly—a Broadway musical theater star. I would lip-sync to musical theater soundtracks in front of the wall-size mirror in our living room before it was even cool to do so. It made me so happy.

I never followed my big dreams. I was too self-conscious and awkward —a sensitive, nervous child. My parents were the only ones on our block who had foreign accents, we were financially unstable, and once my dad died, chaos ensued. I ain't gonna lie: suffering the loss of a parent at a young age screws with you.

Even though I didn't follow my dreams, after several years of scrambling to find my purpose, I did end up getting a dream job.

This is as much my journey as it is yours.

We casting directors have a special relationship with actors, because we are the ones who say, "yes, we want to give you an opportunity because we think you have something special in you, to share with the world." But we say "no" much more than we say "yes."

This book is designed to get you to "yes!"

If you want something, just go for it. Don't settle for the safe way, for "Plan B." Take the path you want most; believe me, you will regret it when you are older if you don't.

—Cathy Reinking, June, 2019

1 BRUTAL HONESTY

Let's get very real.

I've been a casting director since the early '90s. Jeff Greenberg (*Frasier, Modern Family*) gave me my big break. My very first job was as a casting assistant on the NBC show *News Radio* in 1994. That year I also worked on *Wings, Frasier,* and a new show—*The Pursuit of Happiness*—that only lasted one season (if that). It was created by the *Frasier* core team and co-starred Brad Garrett before he booked *Everybody Loves Raymond.* I spent twelve years in the upper echelons of network television, working on shows for nearly all of the biggest (at the time)—NBC, CBS, Fox, The WB, ABC—and under the umbrella of several of the major studios—20th Century Fox, Paramount, Warner Brothers, Sony. Honestly, there were so many I can't even remember them all.

Who knew then that the '90s was the best time to be an actor? There was no social media, no YouTube, no smartphones. We never discussed "influencers" or YouTube stars, and no one cared about how many views they got except as it related to the Nielsen ratings that came out every morning (by the way, the original incarnation of *Arrested Development* had dismal ratings the Monday morning after it premiered).

The '90s were the simple days when actors would come in for an audition and be directed by a casting director who knew the best way to unlock their best work. I was trained to be a theater director at UCLA, so I love working with actors in this capacity (and am particularly good at it, if I do say so myself). Since very few directors on set know how to direct actors, the in-person audition was sometimes the only time the actor was directed and guided to reveal his or her true self in the situation the scene called for. A casting director is the only person who truly knows the style of the project and what the writers, directors and producers like. Actors

2

who coach other actors don't have this knowledge. Acting teachers who have never casted a project don't have this knowledge. Casting directors are a rare breed and should be fully acknowledged for this.

From 1994 to 2005, I worked on thousands of hours of episodic network television (along with a few feature films), and we almost never taped any of the auditions (when we did, it was an extremely rare circumstance). The callbacks were always done live in the room with the writer-producers or director, depending on whether it was for episodic or film.

During that period, I helped hundreds—most likely *thousands*—of actors get SAG and AFTRA work. It was a time when all actors had to do was audition, practice their craft, and do plays.

It was also a time when demo reels contained scenes from episodic shows that aired and films that got distribution. That was all. Actors creating their own scenes for their reels was considered unacceptable.

If you wanted to be an actor, you had to live in either Los Angeles or New York. Those were your choices. We never talked about "local hires." All the actors had to be *actual* local hires, unless they were auditioning for a pilot. With pilots, we had to cast a wider net than just Los Angeles. But usually that wider net was limited to New York City or Chicago.

It was also a time when the term "pilot" only meant one thing: the first episode of an episodic show that may or may not become a series. It was developed under the umbrella of a network and studio and that network paid the tab. If it was picked up by the network, it became a series and the pilot was broadcast. If the series was not picked up, then the pilot went into the black hole of past pilots, usually never to see the light of day. I worked on at least twelve pilots that never went to series; it's heartbreaking for everyone involved.

What infuriates me now is when someone says they are making a pilot (or worse: that they were *cast* in a pilot), but there is no network or studio attached already. Yes, a producer will self-finance a short video in the hopes of selling the idea to a network or cable channel and will call it a "pilot," but it really isn't. When an actor posts or tells me they were cast in a pilot, I always ask, "At what studio?" If they don't know or they explain that it *might* go to Netflix, I have to correct them in order to protect all those actors who book actual pilots. One is more likely to win the lottery than to sell a spec pilot to a network. Don't boast that you booked a pilot and make all your actor friends envious or depressed unless it's the real deal.

The harsh truth is that, with more and more platforms being created and more and more content therefore needed, it's gotten harder for the "working class actor" to make a living and for "nobodies" to break in.

But there is a way to cut through all the noise and make a living as an actor, and this book is intended to help you fulfill your dreams of an acting career.

First off, the acting profession is not a game—it's a profession like any other, and you must look at it that way. Yes, *many* sons and daughters of get hired a lot—Wyatt Russell, Dakota Johnson, John David Washington —but it's not impossible for a "nobody" to get noticed; you just have to be an incredibly creative, resourceful, and passionate "nobody" who thinks outside the box and is willing to do <u>all</u> the work necessary to break into the business, which, nowadays, is like breaking into Fort Knox. If you've seen the CAA building in Los Angeles, you know what I mean; it looks like a fortress, albeit a very architecturally exciting one, but a fortress nonetheless, seemingly designed to intimidate. And it's not just CAA—all the studios are behind huge, intimidating gates.

But it *is* possible to book acting jobs—otherwise, I wouldn't bother writing a third edition. I love, admire, and respect actors very much and want all of you to succeed. You just need to be smart about the journey you have chosen.

The acting profession is not for the lazy or the meek. Just warning you now: talent is one thing, but all the other skills and personal fortitude you have to possess and all the things you must do to get yourself noticed are mind-boggling. You also need to spend a lot of money; with all the expenses an actor has from the get-go—transportation costs (car, gas, maintenance, insurance); housing (rent, utilities); cable or streaming networks (you *must* watch lots of episodic TV); tickets for concerts, theatre and films; headshots; an up-to-date computer; smartphone; video camera; a home self-tape set up or paying to tape with an outside company; classes and coaching sessions; subscriptions to Actors Access and IMDB Pro,; workshops; networking events; office supplies; clothes; grooming; therapy; socializing; airline travel and hotel (if you truly want to be considered a "local hire")—the fact of the matter is it's getting harder and harder to make a profit, especially with all the ultra-low-budget independent projects being made now. These hard truths are distressing, but I feel an obligation to talk about it all—the good, the bad, and the ugly.

Now more than ever, an actor has to see him or herself as an *entrepreneur*. Merriam-Webster defines an entrepreneur as *"one who organizes, manages, and assumes the risks of a business or enterprise."* Later in the book I will discuss at length what it means to be an actor-entrepreneur. On the downside, pursing acting as a profession is a risky proposition. The upside is, you can now take full control of your "business" and not be solely reliant on others to fully express yourself. It's an exciting time for artists, but you must take the bull by the horns… *and tame it.*

5

In this book I will explain, step by step, how you can master the acting profession as well as make a difference in this world. We'll discuss self-tape vs. in-person auditions in detail as well as all the styles of auditioning and acting according to genre. I will also cover where to live as an actor, how to create your own content without breaking the bank, taming your inner saboteur, time management, how to network without it feeling like a chore, how to maintain your enthusiasm, and so much more.

But first things first, what is good acting?

2 WHAT IS GOOD ACTING?

Although this is not a book on acting technique—it's a book on how to audition well—I feel compelled to bring up the subject of good acting and how I can assess an actor's ability in a matter of seconds.

Some great actors have had substantial training and some have not. I am biased toward the well trained theatre actor because I am passionate about theatre and the special devotion it takes to pursue that love. Oddly, there doesn't seem to be a correlation between success as a working actor and training. Actors who graduate from Yale School of Drama (such as Lupita Nyong'o) book jobs and actors who have never had an acting class (Jennifer Lawrence) work regularly in both episodic and film. As long as you're a good, compelling actor, you will book jobs.

I'm fascinated by the intangibles of acting. Whenever I'm emotionally moved by a performer, either on a screen or on a stage, I wonder what it is about this actor that I'm so drawn to. As an actor, you have to find a way to translate your intellectual knowledge into your physical and emotional self. For most actors, this will mean being committed to the study of acting in a class and/or performing in plays. Taking classes and working on the stage will not guarantee you will book jobs in film and episodic television, however. Being a good, compelling actor will.

Good acting is non-acting acting. We—casting directors, directors, producers, writers (and, of course, the audience!)—don't want to see the work. We don't want to see you "act." The transition from you as a person to you as the character should be seamless. When you say your lines, it should seem as if you were having a private intimate conversation, with the audience as the voyeur. There should be no artifice or veneer to the dialogue.

Good acting is from your gut and your heart, not from your head.

Good acting is your ability to reveal many emotions simultaneously in a made-up situation—Stanislavski's "Magic If." If I were a teenaged girl who was forced to go to a conversion therapy camp (the film *The Miseducation of Cameron Post*), how would I feel in this situation? What emotional qualities would I bring to this role? True and deep emotions make you emotionally compelling, and that's what we look for.

A good actor is relatable, likable, natural, and fully connected to the other person. A good actor listens and reacts in the moment to what is going on in the scene. If you're too self-conscious to go to an intimate place, where you really and truly connect with another human being, you will not audition well. If you're uncomfortable with intimacy—if you continually "check out" of the scene when it starts getting good and connected—you will not book work.

Finally, good acting draws us in as if there were a magnetic force field surrounding the actor. It's imperative you find your force field. A good actor is a *charismatic* person.

So how do you stand out from the hordes of other actors vying for the same role? The answer is not what you would think. It's not that you have to come in and be "different" or "make a bold choice" to wake the casting director up from the stupor of having to hear the same material over and over again. "Standing out from the crowd" does not mean using an accent when none is called for or wearing a silly hat. Standing out does not come from the outside but from within. That's one reason it makes me nervous when some acting teachers tell actors to "make bold choices." If you're thinking about how you can be different, your focus is in the wrong place.

You can't obsess over the other actors coming in for the same role either. More often than not when you do get an in-person audition, you'll be sitting in the waiting area with actors you recognize from episodic shows and automatically think they'll get the job over you because they have better résumés than yours or they are better actors than you are. We don't want you to try to be more like them. We're not looking for an "image." As Alex Loyd says in his terrific self-help book, *The Healing Code* (thehealingcode.com), the erroneous precept that "image is everything" originates from the belief that "I'm not okay, and if people get to know me, they will come to that same conclusion, so whatever the cost I need people to see a manufactured me instead of who I really am." Portraying yourself in an inauthentic, pre-packaged way is the worst form of manipulation and we can see right through it.

In truth, you can wow us simply by being yourself. This is true in all auditioning, but especially for episodic TV roles. All we want is you, and to see your authentic, natural charisma coming through the character.

Casting directors are like matchmakers between the director, producer and creator, and the actors. Metaphorically, I ask myself, would I want to date this person? Or just have coffee and look for an excuse to leave? Would I consider a long-term relationship? Marriage? The auditioner who gets the "marriage proposal" is the one who gets the job. In other words, you can't just be "okay" or "fine." You have to be "Wow! This actor must be in the project."

What do we look for? What makes us want to watch a particular actor over another? *Charisma.* Charisma is the bedrock of how we connect with each other as human beings. It's the foundation of how we communicate with each other. Without charisma, without sex appeal, without attraction, without the force and chemistry between people, our lives would be dull and boring as hell. Without charisma, your audition will put us to sleep.

I've come to realize, because of all the hours I've spent in those rooms and watching self-tapes and demo reels, that the key ingredients to the art of charisma are *self-knowledge* and *balance*. In order to tap into the full power of your individual charisma, you absolutely must know who you are and then have the ability to reveal that true self in an audition. If you aren't brave enough to look deep within in order to truly know and accept who you are, then you most likely won't be a very good actor.

Your true self is a reflection of both your dark and light qualities. A charismatic person is the perfect balance of the two. If you are all dark qualities, you will scare us, and if you are all light qualities, we won't be emotionally moved by you. Shakespeare's plays are all about self-knowledge and balance. If you're too much of one thing, you either end up dead or your family is destroyed *(Macbeth, King Lear)*. If you're the perfect balance of man and woman, dark and light, you end up happily married (Rosalind in *As You Like It)*.

You must ask yourself, with honesty and fearlessness, "Who am I? What emotional qualities do I possess?" As an actor, the only thing you can play is emotions. It's the only thing the audience responds to, really. You think we're attracted to hot bodies? No. We're attracted to a strong emotional inner life. Lady Gaga is extremely popular for writing and singing songs that are extremely emotional. Apparently, whether we listen to very happy songs or very sad songs, dopamine is released when we *feel* and either way we are elated by this. *Feeling makes us feel better.*

In embarking on your journey of self-knowledge, try this simple exercise: make a list of who you are emotionally. What are your emotional qualities? How would you describe yourself in one-word descriptions— sad, angry, optimistic, caring, fierce, funny, smart, passionate? Your list should be at least ten qualities long, although fifteen to twenty is best. You should be brutally honest. Who are you really? Are you depressed, melancholy, joyous? Are you skeptical, laid back, romantic? You can have contradictory traits and, in fact, it's best if you do. You can be loving and difficult, angry and peaceful. A complex person is an interesting person. An interesting, fully dimensional actor succeeds in booking the part.

Your list of qualities might look like this:

Dark	Light
Angry	Passionate
Frustrated	Joyous
Sad	Funny
Insecure	Sexy
Bitter	Brave
Fearful	Optimistic

Most people only show one or two of their qualities to folks they are meeting for the first time. The above list I made for myself. I probably only show smart and funny to strangers. I might show four or five qualities (smart, funny, optimistic, brave) to my close friends and six or seven (add in angry and sad) to my mate. When I'm alone in my private space I reveal all of my qualities, especially those I want to hide (bitter, insecure, fearful). Sadly, most people are not expressing to others the full gamut of their emotional lives. My darker qualities are not easy to take but they do make up who I am. They are part of my emotional arsenal. If I'm not expressing my authentic self to the world, I'm cheating my colleagues, friends, and family out of connecting with me on a deep and meaningful level. I'm sure the above describes many if not most people.

...But actors are not most people. *It is your job to connect with other human beings.* It's your obligation to know yourself and have the courage to reveal at least five of your qualities in every audition, every scene, every project. If you're too nervous to reveal yourself the second you walk in the own skin, you won't let us in… and you *need* to let us in. We need to *see* you. You can't be protective of your emotions, especially the darker ones.

The tricky part is that you need to reveal your authentic self the moment we come in contact with you. You can't come in inauthentic or emotionally blocked and then, five minutes into the audition, finally start showing us a glimmer of who you are. There is no "warming up" in an audition or that important meeting with an agent.

That is not to say that if you're an angry person, you should come in showing your anger, or if you're depressed, you should come in wallowing in your angst. You should come into the room in a good place, while remaining emotionally available to us and to the requirements of the scene.

A great audition contains at least five emotional qualities. You can grab what you can from your own personal arsenal and choose what is appropriate for the particular role. For instance, if I were auditioning for a role on *Law and Order: SVU,* I might choose funny, angry, passionate, brave, and sad from my list. If your audition is one note, one emotion—such as sadness—it will be boring. If it's just bitter, it will be indulgent. Human nature is multi-faceted, so your auditions should be, too.

The list you've made of your own emotional qualities is a beautiful tool you can refer to always, even as you revise it. You can go to your darker qualities for the dramatic scenes and the lighter ones for the comedic. You can combine your dark and light qualities for the leading roles in either genre. You can go to your lightest of the light qualities for commercial auditions.

You don't have to bring in anything into the audition that is foreign to you. You don't need to conjure up emotions that you've never experienced. It's all you and it will work for any scene, any role, in all media.

1: Reveal Your 'Natural Sexiness'

Come on, let's face it, there is nothing like looking into your lover's face and seeing his or her eyes look at you in "that way." The eyes are open, relaxed, and thinking only about you in a lovely way. They exude a positive energy—a *desire*—and you can't help but be drawn in. The person who looks at you in that moment is *sexy*, and casting directors are drawn to this natural sexiness as well. We are human, after all. We love actors partly because they *are* sexy. Sexiness is the basis of what makes people attracted to each other in the first place. If you can somehow convey your natural sexiness without being overtly flirty or trying too hard and coming on too strong, you immediately have us in your corner. If you can walk into The Room and look us in the eyes, feeling good, positive, and sexy, we will be excited to experience your audition.

To clarify this point, I am not suggesting that you *come on* to the casting director. I'm not promoting that you dress in a trashy fashion (unless it's called for in the scene, of course), say anything in a provocative manner, or enter expecting to experience the "casting couch" in order to get the role. I am not talking about sexiness in a disrespectful or uncomfortable way. I am talking about one's own innate sexiness that is reflected in the eyes and in one's attitude and confidence level. In essence, I'm talking here about what is at the very core of your charisma. Are you open as a person? Are you accessible? Do you have a natural sex appeal? The more you feel good about yourself, the more your natural sexiness will be revealed to us. That is what we want to see.

What is sex appeal? The French call it having "le chien," which literally translates to "the dog." Sex appeal is something visceral and earthy. It is not really about physical beauty. Look at Frances McDormand. She's not the most beautiful woman, but on film and on stage, we can't keep our eyes off of her. What about Judi Dench, Jeanne Moreau, Angelica Houston, Adam Driver, Paul Giamatti, Sam Rockwell, to name only a few? These actors possess a life force. George Bernard Shaw's heroines possess a life force, which he described as "energy and success, the ideal of the human species." Actors who have sex appeal are the ideals in our society. We idolize them. We pay money to watch them and to read about them!

Actors we idolize embody all that life has to offer—joy, sadness, fear, disappointment, strength, vulnerability—and sometimes they can show this with one look! Daniel Craig comes on screen and we see a whole life in his eyes—which makes him sexy as hell. Kate Winslet does this also. She's gorgeous, yes, but her eyes convey the full gamut of human emotion. She has depth, and nothing could be sexier on screen.

Sexiness is being self-*aware* not self-*conscious*. Sexiness is being comfortable in your own skin. Sexiness is being open and honest about your dark as well as your lighter side.

Which photo is more charismatic? In the first, she is showing fear. In the second, she is relaxed and open, showing her natural charisma.

Again, the photo on the right is charismatic. The one on the left has dead eyes. You'll get nowhere with dead eyes—there's nothing going on behind them.

2: Create Chemistry by Making It About The Other Person

Going back to our dating metaphor, don't be a selfish lover. The scene is not all about you or your character. As in all good scenes, either on stage or on camera, it's about two people connecting through their desire. It is the chemistry between people that makes us want to watch them. What is your relationship to that other person? How do you feel about them? What do you want from them?

If you're acting by yourself we will not be drawn to you. You must connect emotionally with the other person. You must *see* them. You must listen and react to what they're saying to you. You must have a real give-and-take conversation with them. You must honestly talk to them as opposed to acting at them. You must be present in the moment and interested in them. This is what good acting is all about—revealing real human behavior in an unreal situation.

Sometimes you will be auditioning for co-star roles—in fact, a *lot* of the time, as there are more co-star roles written than any other category.

You will come in for the waiter, the cop, or the receptionist. These are the most obvious examples, but, in any scene in which yours is a co-star role, it is definitely not about you or your character. In a comedy especially, you will be the set-up for the joke that the star will deliver. During the audition, if you make the scene all about the waiter or the cop, you will overact and tank. You will stop listening. You will try your hardest to be FUNNY (cue jazz hands)! You will want to make an impression because you will only have three to five lines in the scene. You will want to make the role bigger and more important that it is. But, the co-star role is already important—it is helping to further the story. The producers, who always want to save money, are going to pay an actor a salary to play the role that pushes the story forward. Just keep it real. Listen, talk, and know it's all about the star of the show or movie, not about the funny waiter.

On the left, the actress is trying too hard to be funny. She's pushing the comedy and it doesn't look natural. On the right, she is herself, with good, positive energy. That version is much more likely to get hired.

3: Express Vulnerability

The more we see your vulnerability, your depth, and your reflection of the human condition, the more we are drawn to you. This is true for comic roles; this is true for dramatic roles. And, it is most effective in roles that are unsympathetic—the asshole, the bitch, the villain. If you can find the humanity in these roles, the vulnerability, your audition will have dimension, a "real life" quality, and a *likeability* that will make us want to watch you. If you play the unsympathetic roles on the nose, as a stereotype, we will be bored at the very least and repelled at the worst.

The nicest, most vulnerable actors make the best villains (Alan Rickman in the original *Die Hard* and in the Harry Potter series. Heath Ledger in *The Dark Knight*). Sweethearts make the best bitches (Rachel McAdams in *Mean Girls*, Megan Mullally in *Will and Grace*). If an actual Karen-type had played the role of Karen in *Will and Grace,* the role would have been unwatchable. That character is a drunken, sarcastic, vindictive, and hateful bitch. As played by Megan Mullally, who is one of the sweetest, most grateful actresses in the world, we love her. She played Karen as completely vulnerable.

Amy Pietz *(The Office),* who is an actress with incredible pathos and vulnerability, can play—as she puts it—the most popular character-type written for actresses in their 30s: the "bitchy, conniving, bitter woman." All she has to do is reflect on the times in her own life when she was "bitchy," and—as she so eloquently explained when I interviewed her for the previous edition of this book—those are the times when she is fearful of something. In real life, if she is scared of something, those are the times she will lash out or "bite." When she is asked to play this kind of role, she asks of the character, "what is she the most afraid of?" This leads her to the vulnerable, mushy core of any strident role. This is exactly what Meryl Streep did in *The Devil Wears Prada*, playing what could have been a caricature. The scene in which we see her without her hair coiffed and with no makeup, we see how incredibly fearful and sad she really is, underneath the imperious veneer.

Morally complex antihero roles—such as those played by Jon Hamm *(Mad Men)*, Bryan Cranston *(Breaking Bad)*, Michael C. Hall *(Dexter)*, Edie Falco *(Nurse Jackie)*, and Mary-Louise Parker *(Weeds)*, are absolutely driven by the actor's own vulnerability and innate humanity.

If you allow your vulnerability to show in the sympathetic roles—the lover, the victim, the innocent girl-next-door—not only will you book the job, you will become a beloved star, such as Amy Adams, Scarlett Johansson, Jennifer Lawrence, Michelle Williams, and Ryan Gosling.

Don't be afraid to show us the side of you that you otherwise only show yourself. We all have one public persona and another that we share with our family and friends. The vulnerable you is the real persona, the person you are when you're alone at night in your personal space, stripped of any pretense. That's what we want to see: you, revealed. That's why we go to the movies. That's why I found great solace and escape as a lonely teenager who had just lost her dad. I could stare up at a screen, watching actors reveal to me what I was feeling. It was far too scary a place for me to go by myself. But watching actors go there I could feel safe and was comforted.

Brilliant actors are brave folks. Emotionally, they go where the rest of us are scared to. They speak from the gut. They are not afraid to show the ugly side of humanity, as long as it's real and truthful. They are raw. Ryan Gosling is an example—in everything he does. So are Jeremy Renner *(The Hurt Locker, Avengers)*, Michael Fassbender *(Shame, X-Men)*, Amy Ryan *(Gone, Baby Gone* and *Birdman)* and, of course, Natalie Portman in *Black Swan*. Tommy Lee Jones' sorrow, disappointment, fear, terror, loneliness, strength, and disgust when he learns of his son's secret life and subsequent brutal murder in *In The Valley of Elah* are all revealed silently in his eyes and face. Judi Dench is not afraid to be vulnerable and unappealing. She is astounding in *Notes On a Scandal*. Physically, she is dowdy and old. She wears no makeup, her hair is cropped short, and she

19

plays a woman who is monstrous. But, damn, she is riveting and gorgeous in all her emotional nakedness! Her performance helps me better understand the human condition. I see a side of myself in her; a side that I don't want to admit is there. This is the kind of acting—authentic, audacious, and raw—that makes me physically shake.

These are the performances that earn Academy Award nominations.

How can an actor possibly reveal the human condition in an audition room or, even more challenging, a self-tape? Granted, this is a gargantuan task; but you simply must bring your full emotional life into every audition situation. When you audition for episodic TV dramas and dramatic films, you must go dark and deep with the full gamut of human emotion—pain, loss, fear, disappointment, melancholy, passion, and fierceness. These auditions can't be one or even two notes. They have to be as dynamic as possible. As I stated previously in this chapter, a great audition will be one in which you show at least five different emotions. To make matters even more difficult for you, you can't fake or push the emotions. You can't *act* sad. You have to *be* sad. We have to see it and feel it in your eyes. These auditions are very intimate and yet an audition room or a self-tape is the least intimate and inviting environment there is. You have to come in and immediately "give it all you've got." With self-tapes, you have a limited time in which to create and submit them. There is no time to warm up during your audition. You must already be there—at that revealing, intimate place.

Both actors are revealing an organic vulnerability. They have many emotions going on at the same time—intriguing and compelling.

4: Control The Adrenaline Rush

If you are a person who prays, I would suggest you don't ask for fame, fortune, or even just an acting job. Pray for the ability to be relaxed and centered. If you can master these two issues, everything else you need to succeed will follow.

You will not have a good audition if you're nervous. No one hires someone who is nervous. It is your job to make us comfortable and relaxed. It is your job to entertain us. A great audition happens when we simply sit back and enjoy watching you. If you're nervous, we will feel sorry for you, we will feel compassion toward you, but we will not feel comfortable hiring you and sending you to a sound stage.

A sound stage is an intimidating place. Often the director does not have time to work with you, especially in episodic television, and you will be directed only by the casting director in the audition. The director is worried about the lights, the set, the shot, the story, and a million other things. The actor who is hired must be able to handle him or herself on the set because if you turn out to be the problem, you will be replaced.

21

If you're nervous, you will not be able to take direction. If you can't take direction from the casting director and make an adjustment, then you won't get called back.

If you're tight or blocked when auditioning, you will only be able to do the scene one way: *your* way—the way you rehearsed it. Casting directors —not you or another actor—know what will book the job. We will guide you with great knowledge and expertise because we have been doing this a long time and we want you to do well. We are on your side. We want this role to be cast and we want it to be *you*. If you're nervous and/or resisting the direction, you will lose our interest instantly, and once you lose that, it's hard to get called back in for anything. You have just wasted our time and time is of the essence in casting, especially for episodic TV. Every moment counts, and if you've wasted your precious moment in a casting director's office being nervous, you will regret that for a long time.

If you find yourself in this situation—fighting or resisting the direction, not being able to hear and process the notes quickly and intelligently—try to calm down and listen. Do not think, "Damn, I'm messing up—why can't I get this?" Getting direction is a good thing, not a bad thing. If the casting director did not think you were worth it, he or she would not spend the extra time with you. Remember that when you find yourself tightening up.

There are various things you can do to help with nerves before you get to the audition. You're going in (hopefully!) for roles on the episodic shows you love and in for directors whom you admire. Naturally you're going be nervous. If you're lucky enough to test for a primetime network pilot, you know going in how much money you will be making if you book it. Your life and lifestyle will literally change overnight for the better, and it's easy to lose your focus. I've seen great actors tank in these rooms due to nerves. I've had the heartbreaking experience of watching these great actors with good, strong credits start pushing the comedy when they feel the enormous pressure. What was loose and fun and hilarious in the first audition room now evolves into an audition that is fake and forced, all due to nerves. No matter how good they were in the first auditions, if they can't perform under pressure—when the stakes are very high, in front of the episodic executives—they will not get hired.

Instead of taking Xanax to calm your nerves, as so many actors are prone to do, my suggestion would be to pray for help first and then do the following activities.

Hypnotherapy. This is sort of like accelerated psychoanalysis. Hypnotherapy is great for stage fright, smoking too much, drinking too much, and eating too much—pretty much anything that ails you. I live by it and can tell you firsthand it changed my life. You have to be able to abandon yourself to the hypnotherapist; if you can do this, you will see results right away.

Stephanie Jones, a prominent HypnoTherapist, writes on her website (www.stephanie-jones.com):

> *Hypnosis is a natural state where the critical factor is bypassed, usually through relaxation. This allows healing, pleasing suggestions to be accepted by the subconscious mind, resulting in life-altering, permanent change.*

> *It is a well-known fact that we come to believe and therefore achieve whatever we repeat to ourselves, whether the beliefs are true or false. The subconscious mind cannot tell the difference between a fear-based lie or a joy-filled truth. People become who they are because of their dominant thoughts, the thoughts and beliefs they hold in their subconscious mind. Thoughts become things and events in our lives.*

> *Using the imagination and focused concentration with a hypnotic guide, you can access the beliefs and idea patterns that are held in your subconscious and alter them. Change those thoughts and beliefs to represent your authentic deeper self. Free*

23

yourself from any obsolete belief systems inherited from worn-out voices from the past.

Remember, the subconscious is the single most powerful goal-achieving mechanism known to humankind. Hypnosis allows you to access and reinforce what you want and need on a deep level and therefore manifest it in your life with greater ease.

Meditation. The practice of meditation can be an effective way for actors to combat issues with nerves as well as self-doubt. There was a time, not long ago, when meditation was considered a rarified form of enlightenment, only for gurus, New Agers, and those individuals who had hours on end to tune out the outer world and look inward. Not so now, as it's become commonplace for people of all walks of life and all socio-economic backgrounds to learn the principals of meditating. Classes are available now in every city and in every price range, not to mention the enormous amount of apps *(Insight Timer, Headspace)* that can help you start and maintain your practice.

Meditation has many benefits, including emptying your mind of all the "noise" (inner voices that can be negative), slowing down your nervous heart rate, relaxing your body and face, and centering and focusing your energy. After meditation, the mind is sharper with enhanced creativity and memory. In fact, modern scientific research confirms that regular mediation produces a higher level of happiness and a longer life span.

The following is a simple breathing exercise that can be done before an audition, either at home or in the waiting room:

- Close your eyes and inhale through your nose for a count of eight or ten.

- Hold your breath for an equal duration.

24

• Exhale through the nose for a count of eight or ten.

Repeat above steps three to six times. It's amazing what this very simple exercise can do.

5: All We Want Is You

Casting directors don't care how cute or handsome you are, or who you know who knows so-and-so. If we can't connect with you as a person, we won't be interested in you as an actor. If you enter the audition as a different person than the one you show us in the actual scene, I guarantee we will be more interested in the one who entered first. That is all we want, the *authentic* you in the scene saying the dialogue as you in the situation specified in the script. It helps if you're a good person to begin with.

If you have a chip on your shoulder and you're in a negative personal zone, we will sense that right away and turn off to you. As discussed previously, if you're nervous and emotionally blocked, you won't be able to take direction. You—the real you—must remain relaxed, malleable, and easy to work with. Again, let's go back to the dating metaphor: do you want to marry someone who's not genuine? Who's emotionally blocked? Afraid to reveal themselves? Heck no.

6: Be A Good Listener

You've heard it a million times, but I might as well remind you: **acting is reacting and good acting is listening.** Film or episodic television acting is not about you pontificating or talking into the air, it is about you listening to what the other person has to say as if for the first time. We need to see the reaction register on your face and specifically in your eyes *as you are listening*, and then we need to hear the line or reaction. It happens

25

in a nanosecond. But without seeing how the other person's words *affect* you, the scene will have no life to it. It will just be you regurgitating your lines at the proper times.

We need to hear the cue, see the reaction, and feel the response.

Beware of overreacting. You can't act the reaction; you have to think it. If you're truly present, in the moment and listening, then your reaction will be natural and beautiful. It is the reaction that moves us. We want to see how you're affected. It is in that spark that magic happens.

The last thing we want to see is you acting. Good on-camera acting is non-acting acting. If we can tell that you're acting, we will want to flee the audition room or turn off that self-tape. We just want the real you, talking to us. That's all the scene usually is, just two (or perhaps a few more) people talking to each other. We want you to talk to us, not act as if you're the only one working. It's not "work." It's just a conversation.

7: Show Humility

You hear of cocky actors who take advantage of their fame. You hear of stuck-up actresses who obsess about their looks and complain about their weight and age. Don't be one of these. In your darker moments, you imagine that the actor with the largest ego, who is the most arrogant, gets the job. Believe me, they don't. Especially as a young actor who is just making the audition rounds, you must not allow yourself to try masking insecurity with cockiness. Just like in dating, that is one of the biggest turn-offs there is. Be confident, not arrogant. There is a huge difference. Confidence is having a sure sense of yourself; feeling comfortable in your own skin. Arrogance is when you do not feel sure of yourself but you act as if you do.

26

David Hyde Pierce, to me, is the epitome of the humble actor. Not only is he an excellent actor, he is also one of the most gracious, generous, humble people I have met in all of my travels. He is saintly, in fact, and grateful for all the good fortune that has come his way. To me, he is the ideal actor and ideal human being, and if all of us could be like him, the world would be a better place.

It is true, alas, that there are a lot of cocky actors and actresses out in the world. But the truly humble and gracious actors will get the lasting attention of the casting directors.

If you're not feeling secure with yourself, take classes, go into therapy, do anything, but don't carry the baggage that you're "all that" into the audition or on your self-tape.

On the other end of the spectrum, there are very good actors who don't want to come off as cocky, so they err by being so humble that they make themselves invisible. Their inner dialogue is one of "I don't want to be a needy actor so I will act as if I don't need the casting director at all." In this case, the actor comes off as apathetic or, worse, aloof. Trying to make yourself invisible is just as arrogant as trying to make yourself more important than you are. It is putting on a façade that prevents us from seeing who you really are and the façade is just a mask for deep insecurity.

8: Don't Think So Much

There is nothing that kills an audition faster than actors analyzing their work as they're doing it. Good acting does not come from your intellect; it comes from your gut. It's great to prep a scene and understand what it's about, what you want in the scene, what is your subtext, your back story, etc. But when you actually audition in person or on a self-tape, the scene must be done as if you're saying those words in that situation with that other person for the first time. There has to be spontaneity to the scene, otherwise it will be too studied—too rehearsed. It will not have a life of its own.

Also, and more importantly, if, as you're doing the scene, you're having an inner dialogue—"God, I blew that line," "Damn, it went better as I was doing it on the drive over here," "How come I'm not connected?"— you will kill your chance of booking the job. The camera lens and those on the other side of the table in the room see it all. We see when you drop out of the scene. We can tell when you're not fully present in the moment. We can tell when you don't even believe in what you're saying, when you're self-conscious.

I'm not saying you shouldn't prepare a scene. In fact, it's only when you have fully prepared a scene that you get out of your head. And I don't mean memorize the lines on the page or analyze it until you've taken all the life out of it. It's not that mechanical. You have to work on the audition scene until it is fully in your bones, until you begin feeling emotions within the scene, and until it seems like a normal conversation with normal reactions. "Acting" a scene will most definitely kill an audition. We don't want to see the wheels turning.

Your head has to get out of the way during your audition. You have to abandon yourself to the scene, because only then can you fly.

9: Don't Try So Hard To Be A Leader

This precept pretty much relates to everything in your life. Try too hard and you will just get tired. I learned the hard way that working harder does not mean you will automatically get the job or make more money. Many thought of me as the hardest working casting director in Los Angeles. I always took this to be a good thing. I worked 24/7, was always there for my producers no matter what the time of day; was always there for actors, seeing theatre and running workshops on my nights and weekends. I did have a great reputation, but I burned out. My life became unbalanced and I became unhealthy.

It's possible to work too hard, and, as it relates to auditioning, if your audition *looks like* you're working too hard, you will not get the job. Your audition should appear easy. Great athletes make their work seem easy. Great speakers, politicians, and lawyers make what they do seem easy, as if they're in full and complete command of the situation. Your job as an actor is to allow the words, the emotion, and the humor to just pour out of you naturally, as if you're in a normal conversation. You must do this whether the scene is comic or highly dramatic, even if you have to cry in the scene. You cannot appear indulgent or straining for the emotion in any way. Your audition has to appear organic, natural, as if you're truly in that moment with those feelings, as if it would appear in real life. Acting is nothing but a slice of real behavior. It cannot appear as acting; it has to appear as real. This advice applies to starring as well as smaller co-starring roles.

Casting directors use the expression "small-role fever" to describe what afflicts actors coming in for co-star roles who are trying too hard to make a big impression. A good example of small-role fever is the actor who comes in for the cop role dressed in full cop regalia: uniform, badge and prop gun. Some stereotype the character, using a New York accent when it's not called for, just to appear more cop-like. Other than cops in something like a *Saturday Night Live* sketch, cops are real people; and when we want a cop in an episodic show or a film, it's usually a real one. Just be yourself. All we want is you in that situation as if it were really happening.

In fact, I will go so far as to suggest that you ignore all character descriptions for the co-star roles. Those descriptions are usually written in haste and will be very one-note—angry cop, bitchy trophy wife, bratty teenager. Although you will probably never hear this, co-star roles need to be fully dimensional human beings. They are never stick figures. Don't play a stick figure. Be a person.

An actor needs to take classes, see lots of theatre and movies, and watch a lot of episodic TV. You must exercise religiously, do yoga, and be well groomed. You must constantly work on yourself: you are your commodity. But don't work yourself into the ground and make yourself unbalanced. This brings me to the final tip…

10: Be Healthy Emotionally And Physically

Let's be honest here. For most of us who go into the performing arts, one or more of the following are true:

- We are very emotional (it's what makes an actor very good and can drive the layman insane).

- We grew up in a dysfunctional family.

- We like to party.

- We are trying to compensate for something pretty huge that has been missing since childhood.

- We were ridiculed as kids

- We want to succeed at all costs.

The entertainment business is a selfish lover. It requires all of you. The hard fact is you must put it above all else, especially when you're starting out. It must come before family, before lovers, and before *you*. And, putting it above you is where the trouble can begin.

In order to be around for the long haul, you must be healthy in every way. If you have not been in therapy, start immediately. If you drink too much or take drugs, stop right now. If your methods of dealing with the stress of the business are destructive and escapist, find better ways to cope. If you have crippling insecurity (and believe me, most of us do), start hypnotherapy today. If you're going out after the shows every single night and partying, try to go out just three times a week. If curtailing your partying is too difficult for you, go to therapy for that. Don't use the excuse you can't afford therapy. If you can't afford it, then you probably can't afford pursuing your dreams.

Go into rehab if you have to.

Eat right. Exercise regularly. All the recommendations that doctors have been making for years? Do all of them. The ideal actor is an ideal person. You are the representative of humanity. All walks of life look up to you. They all want to be you. Despite the fact that government money for the arts is not there in abundance, all of society admires you, is entertained by you, would not be able to function without theatre, film, episodic television, webcasts, videos, and musical performances. Life would be a dull place indeed without you. You have a responsibility toward yourself, your fellow actors, and all of mankind.

A casting director can tell the moment you walk in the door whether you're abusing alcohol or drugs. Addictions permeate our society. Self-destruction is all too common. Don't destroy yourself. If you're an addict of any kind, you will destroy yourself when you make a lot of money. Money magnifies who you are at your core. If you're a good person at your core, then money will increase your altruism. If you're a bad person at your core, then money will kill you.

3 THE DIFFERENT STYLES OF AUDITIONING

You are certainly well aware that there are various types of episodic shows, films, web series, and streaming. Do you know that each type has a very specific set of audition rules? Auditioning for a multi-cam sitcom is very different from auditioning for a crime drama. Auditioning for an R-rated comedic film is very different from auditioning for a rom-com.

As soon as you get an audition, you must find out exactly what style the project is. This is critical information because you might get only one shot with a casting director or one self-tape. Any audition for a primetime network, cable episodic show, or prestige streaming platform is too precious to jeopardize by floundering with the material. You don't have time to learn by trial and error. Plus, with self-tapes, you won't ever get the feedback you need to get it right.

Although casting directors often teach acting on the side, the audition room is not the place for us to do so. There is no time. Our job in that context is to fill the roles in a particular film or episodic show. If casting directors had all the time in the world, we could easily spend twenty minutes with each actor, directing you, teaching you how to audition better, giving you feedback, being loving and generous with our knowledge and experience. But there is never enough time in the casting process, especially in episodic, where we need you to come in fully prepared, owning the role, and simply being brilliant. We are not teachers in this context and you should not expect us to be.

Occasionally, you may find a casting director willing to spend lots of time with you. Some casting directors are generous with their feedback and will let you know where you stand in relation to the other actors vying for your role. But very few. Remember, we love actors—you've got something we don't have and most likely can never attain. We are voyeurs and you're our window into the soul. Some casting directors turn that love and admiration into jealously and, frankly, use their power to make you feel miserable. There are toxic casting directors and nice casting directors, and it's imperative that you have the ability to deal with both in any situation, no matter how you're feeling that day. You must learn to deal with difficult people. It's easy for you to get sucked into their energy because you need their approval so badly. Avoid this energy drain at all costs. Be sure of yourself, come in prepared, and never come in needy or desperate.

The following tips were formulated through decades of watching auditions run by the best casting directors in town, running countless auditions myself, and directing thousands of actors. I very often molded their auditions to help them book the job. This insider information is not available from other actors, acting coaches, or even producers or directors, unless they have served as casting directors at some point. An actor is a special type of person; acting is a mysterious talent. *Most folks do not know how to handle or communicate with you.* The better casting directors do.

1: Multiple-Camera Sitcoms

These shows rehearse for five days before shooting in front of a live audience with four cameras. The most famous ones are *I Love Lucy* (which originated the multiple-camera system), *Cheers, Frasier, Friends,* and *Will and Grace.* The multi-camera coverage simultaneously collects four different angles as the scenes play out, usually on a sound stage. It's shot in front of an audience who sit on bleachers much like a little league baseball game and get "warmed up" by a comic. It's a lot of fun to take part in, both as an audience member and as an actor.

A sitcom is the only type of episodic show that rehearses the same script for four days and shoots on the fifth. The director blocks the show much like a play—giving the actors their movements and activities—and there are run-throughs of the whole script for the writer/producers at the end of each day. After the run-throughs, the actors go home and the writer/producers go back to the writers' room and revise the script, sometimes late into the night.

Most of the other episodic shows do not rehearse at all nor rewrite on a daily basis. This is also the only type of episodic show where the actors take off every fourth week. It's a great schedule for actors.

Multi-cam sitcom material must be performed letter-perfect. You cannot paraphrase. You cannot add "ahs" or "ums." You cannot invert a line. If you do so, you will destroy its rhythm and sabotage the delivery the writers painstakingly labored to achieve. Think of it as witty repartee in a Noel Coward play. You would not paraphrase Coward's lines. It is all about rhythm and comic timing. Change the syntax or the punctuation of the line and you destroy it. It should be quick and witty, like the dialogue in a Judd Apatow comedy. You cannot take too much time within the scene. Once it slows down, you will kill the energy. The lines need to overlap each other, like a funny conversation in real life.

As I said previously, the writer in multi-camera sit-com is the producer. Generally, your callback will be in front of the episode's writers, and changing their lines will piss them off.

The energy you bring into the audition should be bright, but not *too* bright. Don't try to be too funny. If you have a natural sense of humor and you stick to the words, it will be funny. Let the words do the work for you. If you try to be funny, it will seem forced and we will just roll our eyes and go on to the next person. If you don't have a natural sense of humor, then you're not going to thrive in sitcoms anyway.

I cut my teeth in the sitcom world and was witness to countless auditions in which actors would try to make their auditions unique by adding an accent or creating a larger-than-life character that was a caricature. Some actors used strange gestures in order to make the material funnier. Some wore funny glasses or a funny tie. These tactics always flopped.

A successful audition for sitcoms requires intelligence, excellent timing, precision, clarity, and a comprehensive grasp of the language. Nothing more, nothing less.

And a word of warning, given from the heart: when you're booked on a sitcom, you must bring your "A" game from that moment on—to the table read, rehearsals, and, of course, shoot days. You can't be too casual on the set with the rest of the cast just because the series regulars are acting like it's no big deal. They're under contract, secure in their jobs on the show, and often won't know their lines until the day of the shoot. You, on the other hand, are a visitor in their world. You must be a perfect person and know your lines, even when they change constantly. You must not challenge the director, ask too many questions, or be too friendly with the stars. I've seen too many actors get recast, sometimes for silly reasons. They can replace you quickly and easily, and will do so if they don't like something you're doing, even if it has nothing to do with your acting.

I would often get calls from set. In one case, the assistant director complained to me of an actor who was making personal phone calls from the set phone (a quaint notion now, of course). In another instance, I got a call from the show runner (the writer-producer assigned to run all aspects of a show) about an actress with an overblown opinion of herself, refusing to eat with the extras, sitting on people's laps, and being a little too friendly. I joked with this show runner by saying, "So, should I give each actor a personality test before I send them to the stage?" The answer was "*yes*." The casting director is responsible for not only the actor's talent but for the actor's attitude and work ethic. It is the casting director whom the producer or assistant director is going to hold responsible for the actor.

You auditioned successfully and booked a job. Please be a perfect human being on the set.

2: One-Camera Comedies

One-camera comedies, sometimes referred to as "single-camera sitcoms," like *Arrested Development, Black-ish,* and *Modern Family,* are also shot in five days, but they are shot like short indie films and usually directed by the hottest indie film directors. They endure hectic shoot schedules with long days and no time for rehearsal. They are shot out-of-sequence—like films are—and it's easy to get lost in the mayhem. You most likely will not get too many notes from the director if you get any at all, and you can't wonder how you're doing. If you're obsessed with thoughts such as "do they like me," you will take your concentration away from the task at hand and fall short of being what they need: a good actor who requires no attention. The director and crew have a lot on their minds, from the script to the lighting to the camera angles; you name it, they're thinking about it. They are not thinking about you... unless you're a problem, in which case they will be irritated by you and may ultimately replace you.

All you have to do is repeat what you did in the audition that earned the job in the first place and take whatever notes they do give you. Do not ask too many questions and don't question the notes. This is a fast and furious train ride, and they don't have time to stop for anyone, especially an actor.

The audition style for the one-camera comedy is tricky. It's not as cut-and-dried as with the sitcom. It's not witty repartee. It's just funny in an idiosyncratic way. You need to bring your own individual idiosyncratic self into the audition without trying to be funny.

The are several types of one-camera comedies, and each one of those sub-genres require subtle differences in the acting. The "mockumentary" *(The Office, Modern Family)* where the conceit is that some unnamed camera crew has parked their cameras in either someone's workplace or home and they're capturing real people in real situations, revealing both humor and pathos. We, the audience, laugh because we recognize our own boring, stupid lives in this world. The humor is found in the thought processes you reveal and not so much in what you say. The comedy needs to be played with great subtlety. After all, for most of these shows, the sides you will be asked to prepare are short, often featuring incomplete thoughts and staccato rhythms. They are not like scenes from a play, or even from a sitcom, where there is a normal exchange between one or more people with some momentum within the scene. There is usually no beginning, middle, or end to the scene, which might be only five lines long. The comedy of the mockumentary one-camera show is in the style and the situation, not in the jokes. You will not be the set-up of a joke that the star will deliver. The language is not witty. You might have one line here and one line on the next page, with a silent bit at the end of the scene in reaction to what the star has just said or done in the situation. You can find humor in the silent reaction to what the other characters are saying. You can find humor in just a look or in the quality you bring to the audition—the *non-verbals*.

I was fortunate to have worked as Manager of Casting at NBC during the pilot season that produced *The Office,* a remake of a British show. I was tasked with overseeing the casting of the pilot. The network test for the final casting of that show was one of the first test auditions that was not done in person. All the actors were videotaped the night before, each singly revealing themselves into the camera lens as their respective characters, each with their own (brilliant) monologue. Jenna Fischer's audition tape still stands out to me, 15 years later, speaking directly to the camera as Pam, revealing her secret desire to illustrate children's books but instead stuck answering phones for a paper supply company in Scranton, PA. The note she was given by one of the producer-writers right before her audition was "don't be afraid to bore us." She didn't need to embellish or complain or role her eyes. She just needed to be in the moment, feeling what the character was feeling, which was sadness, frustration, longing, hope, despair, intelligence—all very subtle, real, and with her natural quirkiness. We, in the network test, watching the video recording, laughed at the sadness of Pam's life, and a new episodic star was born.

Another type of one-camera comedy is the quirky, dysfunctional family saga with wry narration and hilarious asides and inserts. *Arrested Development* is in this category and seemed completely fresh when it debuted in 2003. I was very fortunate to have worked on the first season of *Arrested Development*, right before Marc Hirschfeld, who was then VP of Casting at NBC, asked me to come work at the executive offices at that network. I was sad to leave *Arrested*—it was an extraordinary show to work on at the time with the wonderful Mitch Hurwitz at the helm—but when Mark called I had to accept. In shows like *Arrested Development*, some of the characters are over the top—Gob (Will Arnett), Buster (Tony Hale), Lucille (Jessica Walter)—and some are "normal"/voices of reason —Michael (Jason Bateman), George-Michael (Michael Cera), and Maeby (Alia Shawkat). This is true for the day-players and recurring roles as well. Over-the-top characters—Kitty (Judy Greer), Lucille 2 (Liza Minnelli)— and normal folks —Steve Holt (Justin Grant Wade) and Rocky McMurray (Warden James Buck).

The same is true on comedies as varied as *Black-ish* and *Atypical*. A co-star or guest star on these shows can be over the top or they can be very "normal," very real. As with the mockumentary style, there are no "jokes" *per se,* only situations and wry asides or inserts as part of the narration. How would you fit in? By being a strong actor with superb instincts, knowing when to be broad and when to be natural, but always revealing your quirky sense of humor.

Superstore, The Good Place, Brooklyn 9-9, Barry and *Veep* are all one-camera comedies but have no narration and no one is fake-filming the cast as part of a documentary. *Superstore* has larger-than-life characters but the two leads (America Ferrera and Ben Feldman) are "normal," very similar to a comedic film. In *Veep,* the lead (Julia Louis-Dreyfus) is larger-than-life while all her staff seem real, some almost like in a drama. *Barry* has situations like in a drama (murder and mayhem) but plays like an absurd comedy with a leading man (Bill Hader) who never plays for laughs. On the contrary, he always seems like he's depressed or on the verge of killing someone. It's a tightrope walk of a performance.

The "slice of life" comedies like *Insecure, Shrill, Better Things, Atlanta* and *Ramy* hardly seem like comedies, as they often bring me to tears! They are played for real and the viewer is a voyeur. Often, they deal with serious subjects. The scenes in these shows tend to be longer, not as truncated as most of the other one-cameras I've mentioned. Getting an audition for one of these types of shows must be a joy. In these types of comedies, they are looking almost exclusively for natural and real.

In fact, the expansion of cable and streaming networks, where the subject matter for its scripted shows is far more complex than for network television, it's never been as hip to look less-than-perfect as it is right now. The shows have become more like European films and television shows, where the world depicted is not just populated by beautiful people. I love seeing a "plus size" actress like Aidy Bryant *(Shrill)* play the lead, and the bravery of Lena Dunham *(Girls)* to display her un-supermodel-like naked body in sex scenes. She helped demolish all the rules of episodic casting and I find that very exciting. What matters in cable and streaming shows, above type, is that the acting be superb.

So many great one-camera comedies dot the landscape, it's really hard to keep up. But keep up with them you must. You never know when you'll be asked to audition and you must absolutely know the specific style of the show you are auditioning for.

Suffice it say, there are really no "entry level" roles on these types of comedies. Casting directors who work on these sophisticated, bawdy, smart, goofy comedies must always be on the lookout for comic geniuses. We look for those actors who have a solid comic persona that make us laugh the moment they start to talk. They make us laugh because it's quirky, grounded, vulnerable, recognizable and strange, all at the same time. Having improv experience is pretty much a must now on your résumé for us to even consider you. We also look for actors, however, who can make us cry with their rawness, depending on the style of the show.

Now, more than ever, there is an opportunity for all types of actors to find good roles. You absolutely do not have to audition trying to be someone you're not. You don't have to change a thing. Just come in as yourself, quirks and all. In fact, the quirkier the better.

SPECIAL NOTE: If you've been given sides for an episodic comedy, either in a workshop or for an audition of a show you've never heard of, an easy way to tell whether the show is a multi-camera or one-camera is by the line spacing of the dialogue. Multi-camera comedies are double spaced, single camera are single spaced.

3: Saturday Night Live

Saturday Night Live is the great grandpa of the sketch comedy show and really the only show of this format on network TV. The style of performing on this type of show requires a completely different set of acting skills than the others. It is on the sketch comedy shows that you can finally be all-out FUNNY! You can be outrageous, push-the-envelope, do impressions, and use silly fake accents. In fact, you are encouraged to do so. Your improv skills have to be phenomenal. You have to be quick on your feet, incredibly creative, free, loose and willing to do anything with no semblance of self-consciousness. You have to be willing to go where no normal person can go. This abandon is what has made Will Ferrell a star. He goes places with his acting that we, the normal Joes of the world, would only be able to do drunk.

The actors who get hired on SNL are usually found at *The Groundlings* (based in Los Angeles), *Second City* (based in Chicago), and *Upright Citizens Brigade* (based in both Los Angeles and New York). In fact, UCB is probably the current global epicenter of comedy. The comic actors they look for already have a large body of work with many characters they self-created, refined in countless improv and sketch classes as well as on performance spaces all over the country. Atlanta has several of these spaces that get scouted—Dad's Garage, Laughing Skull, Village Theater—and might become the country's next comedy hotspot. They also scout for talent on the web, endlessly looking at videos for the next great SNL star. There are definitely no "entry level" slots on SNL.

4: New Media

Although Netflix and Hulu, for instance, are streaming on the web, these are not considered "new media." The New Media Agreement under SAG-AFTRA covers small productions, including content like webisodes, reality television shows and motion pictures initially released online (which means this does not cover films meant for film festivals). As it is a category on your resume, it's good for you to know what types of content belong in that section.

New media is mainly self-produced content with no (or micro) budget. The projects are predominantly comic in nature. The acting on this web content is not great, especially for the smaller roles, but these projects can be fun, raw, and really just there for mindless entertainment value. Just look at the early videos Donald Glover produced and you'll see what I mean.

What is the style of acting for this content as far as auditioning? It's the wild west, meaning no rules apply. You can either stick with what you know (good preparation, connecting with your scene partner) or you can wing it. Doesn't matter. That's why the quality of this content suffers, so beware before you commit to a project in this category.

I'm a big believer that actors create their own content vs. working with someone you don't know, that way you have full-control of the quality and you know you will get the footage.

The real beauty of self-produced web-based product is that creative young actors and writers can "put on a show" for very little money… and actually get seen! A lot of folks have gotten paid work this way. That's how Issa Rae, Ilana Glazer and Abbi Jacobson found success, to name only a few.

What casting directors and producers are looking for now are actor/performers who already have a following. They are looking for actors who already have a distinct comic persona and point-of-view so that they can basically plug them into a comedy show and have a fully formed comic character… with a built-in audience to boot.

How can *you* create and refine a comic persona that you can use over and over again in every audition, for every role, whether it be for a multi-camera sitcom, one-camera comedy, web series, or sketch/improv show even? Better yet, how can you create a comic persona that you can make the lead in your own show? First and foremost, you have to know who *you* are. You can't refine who you are if you are always trying to be someone you are not, thinking that's the way to get others to like you. In the audition room or on a self-tape, you can't give us what you think we want, you have to give us *you*, at your core... and perhaps a bit heightened. If, for example, you are not naturally deadpan, you can't do what Aubrey Plaza does (and does so brilliantly)—it will come off as fake and actor-y.

Rachel Bloom became a huge success by creating a comic persona that is basically her, heightened. She's neurotic, insecure, sexy, honest, self-aware, depressed, and joyous. She got on network episodic by creating her own comic music videos (which reflected her comic persona) and releasing them on the web. Prior to her comic videos, she was head writer and director of NYU's premier sketch comedy group while a student there, and performed with UCB in both New York and Los Angeles, so Bloom is the epitome of the go-getter actor/performer. Frankly, it's getting harder and harder to book anything substantial without this kind of drive.

So to start on the road to creating a comic persona that is organic to you, you must ask yourself "Who am I?" You must answer this question with honesty and fearlessness. What emotional qualities do you possess? The great thing about emotional qualities is that they can be contradictory. In fact, such contradiction helps create the best comic personas. Mindy Kaling is sexy and goofy, confident and insecure.

Refinement doesn't come overnight, it takes a lot of work, discovery, insight, fearlessness, and a damn good sense of humor—*your* humor.

5: Comedic Films vs. Episodic Comedy

The world of a comedic film is outrageous and larger-than-life. The world of a episodic comedy reflects the real day-to-day world as we know it. When the leads on a sitcom go out to dinner, they go to a real restaurant with real waiters. When the leads in a comedic film go out to dinner, they usually go to a strange, hyper-real restaurant with goofy waiters.

In a comedic film, the leads are normal people in a world that is wacky. The school that Beanie Feldstein and Kaitlyn Dever (both funny but normal teens) attend in *Booksmart* is populated by over the top stereotypes who wreck havoc on the two leads. Graduation night festivities provide an out-of-control world that would make any parent shudder at the alcohol and drug-induced mayhem that ensues. You would not find that same party in an episodic comedy. Films are more our nightmares and dreams, while episodic is more our everyday life. In a sitcom, the leads are quirky in a normal world. They are more like *us* in a world that is not scary or intimidating. Jim Parsons and the *Big Bang Theory* guys work as engineers and scientists in what might be closer to the real Cal Tech in Pasadena than we might think. Kaley Cuoco works in what appears to be a real Cheesecake Factory and although the brilliant Melissa Rauch as Bernadette is quirky and funny as hell with her high squeaky voice, innocent large eyes and enduring smile, her character as written would not appear in, say, *I Love You, Man.* Would Michael Cera be at home on a multi-camera sitcom? Probably not. He has made his career in one-camera comedies and comedy films. And would Jim Parsons be as huge a star if he had taken, for instance, all of Paul Rudd's roles? My guess is no.

A comedic actor needs to know his strengths in relation to which style is best suited to his sensibilities, demeanor and training. Jim Parsons has an MFA in acting from University of California, San Diego. Michael Cera took improvisation classes in Second City Toronto. Seth Rogan, who has never appeared on a multi-camera sitcom, cut his comedy teeth doing stand-up as a teenager. He has no formal training as an actor. Seems to be an interesting pattern emerging. Since multi-camera shows are most like theatre, this makes sense.

A comedic actor who wants to work in films also has to know and be completely honest with his comfort level in relation to nudity, foul language, drug taking, and extreme sexual content. I don't think the R-rated comedies that push the envelope of bawdy behavior further and further with every film feel like they are going away any time soon.

Melissa McCarthy seems to be able to do it all. She started her career as a stand up and her first big role on episodic was in an hour dramedy *(Gilmore Girls)*. She has been nominated (with a surprise Emmy win in 2011) for several awards for a multi-camera episodic show *(Mike and Molly)*, a sketch show *(Saturday Night Live)*, and two films *(Bridesmaids* and *Can You Ever Forgive Me)* that all definitely pushed the boundaries of proper behavior and the line between comedy and tragedy. She was as real and down-home as one can be on *Mike and Molly* and she is also comfortable with over-the-top antics in both comedic films and sketch comedy. She goes where no man or woman in my real world would dare go and she does it with infectious abandon. She's relatable, real, natural, vulnerable, and never forces the humor.

Across the board, with few exceptions, episodic producers and film directors want acting that is natural—not forced or superficial. Whether it is wacky or real, keep it grounded, connected, and based in human behavior.

6: Hour Dramas

Hour dramas are shot in eight days with at least two days off (usually the weekend) within a seven-day week. They do not take off weeks within the shooting season the way sitcoms do. They are shot exactly like movies, with the same attention to the details of lighting, camera angles, and design. The days on an hour drama shoot are endless. If you're on the crew of an hour drama, you will seldom or ever see your family during the entire season. If you're the lead on an hour drama, the family back home will need to be very patient and understanding because they're going to be without you. These shows are all-consuming and, sadly, not the greatest of fun. If you get to be a series regular on this type of show you will make a lot of money, so you will likely overlook the downside. A lot of actors who work as series regulars on hour dramas call this type of job the "golden handcuffs."

Just as with the episodic comedies, there are stylistic variations to the dramas. As is true for all auditions, know the style of hour drama you are auditioning for.

A serious crime drama, thriller, horror, sci-fi or fantasy (*Chicago PD,* the *American Crime, Homecoming* with Julia Roberts, *The Killing, Manifest*) requires you to get very dark and personal, and to reveal all of yourself. You must act without any pretense. Imagine auditioning for the role of a rape victim on *Law and Order*—you cannot "act" rape victim. You must *be*. And, while that is an intimate, scary place to go, go there you must.

In a show like *Manifest,* you have to make us believe all this crazy stuff is happening and it's dead serious.

Unless it's a scene of great urgency, don't rush it. Let the scene breathe. Take your time. The thoughts that emerge on your face and in your eyes are what will move us, not what you say. The subtext is where the drama lies. Ask yourself, "what am I feeling at the top of the scene" rather than, "how shall I play this?" You can't play a result, you can only play emotions. But they must be organic, real.

If a scene requires that you cry, don't *push* the emotion—especially in an audition or in a self-tape. It will come off as overacting. You have to *actually go there* emotionally. If you can't do this easily, then practice until you can. Tape yourself every day using all kinds of material. It's FREE and should be like going to the gym—a regular practice. I find many actors emotionally blocked, especially the men. Without vulnerability, your scenes will land like an anvil.

In what might seem like contradictory advice, I also believe that if one can find some little bit of humor in a heavy scene, it makes the scene more human and convincing. It brings a semblance of real life to the heavy drama.

Some dramas, such as *MacGyver* or *NCIS: Los Angeles* have a humorous slant. Your role might be one of the comedic elements. If so, you need to bring a heightened version of yourself, as you do with comedy, to the audition. But grounded. Always grounded.

Auditioning for the dramedies is much like auditioning for comedic films. The roles and situations—à la *The Orville,* are heightened in a comedic, daffy way. The roles are all a little larger-than-life, but, as with the traditional episodic comedies, the only acting style the writer/ producers want to see is *natural.* If you go in there and try to be funny and over the top, they will turn off to you immediately. You have to let the dialogue do the work for you. You can't add on another layer of funny. Just be you, a bit of heightened energy, saying those words in that situation.

Shows like *The Resident, This is Us, New Amsterdam* and *How to Get Away with Murder* are high-quality shows in which real people face extraordinary circumstances in a real world. As always, just bring yourself with at least five different emotions within the scene the make sense, yes even if it's a co-star role. Don't embellish it more than that.

With the onslaught of cable and streaming shows comes the onslaught of TV-MA ("mature audiences") content. In order to audition for these hundreds of shows (thousands it seems now), you must be comfortable with material that might involve profane language, highly charged sexual content, and extremely dark themes. I don't believe an actor should compromise his or her moral center, not even for an acting job. But if you decline many of these audition opportunities, your agent might not be happy with you. You will also be limiting your chances of booking work. Please have an open and honest conversation with your representation. Also, please dig deep in your soul and decide what you are willing to compromise and what you aren't. If you have to compromise too much, this might not be the profession for you.

7: Dramatic Films

The "rules" for auditioning for dramatic films are pretty much the same as for dramatic episodic TV. Dramatic episodic is like watching a film every week with the same cast for months. So dig deep and really feel what's going on. Express the trials and tribulations of a person in a way that is relatable, believable, true, authentic, natural, organic.

8: Commercials

During my years casting episodic TV and films in Los Angeles, I never once cast a commercial. It's rare that a casting director on either coast juggles "theatrical" casting (meaning episodic and film) with the casting of commercials. They are usually two different worlds with different agents, agencies, clients, and processes.

From 2006 to 2010, I helped run a casting company in Denver, Colorado, with Sylvia Gregory (Reinking-Gregory Casting) and we pretty much covered all of Colorado. Since there are no episodic shows produced in that state and the film work was rather limited and low paying, we mainly cast commercials. We worked on regional commercials, such as for the Colorado Lottery (which were a lot of fun!) and Banner Health, and we worked on national commercials for clients such as Honda, Duracell, Nike, and Furniture Row.

There is an art to auditioning and working in commercials, and in no way can an actor book a commercial without talent and charisma and all the other elements that have been discussed in this book so far. It makes me nervous when a newbie will say off-handedly, "Oh, I'll just get work in commercials and voice-overs if all else fails." Booking acting jobs is hard no matter what the medium is you're auditioning for.

The following are what I consider the three basic jobs to be found on-camera in commercials:

Spokespeople. These jobs can range from walking around a furniture display, explaining the good deal and excellent design elements to be found in the merchandise of this particular store, or it can be the character of Flo in the Progressive car insurance ads, who has now become a national icon. A good spokesperson is hard to find. You have to make rather dry material, such as the stats of a car engine, sound natural and conversational. You have to take sentences that you would never say in real life and make them warm and accessible. You have to be enthusiastic about the product but you can't *sell*. A common note a client in the audition room will give an actor is "tell, don't sell." If you're stiff and not revealing your personality in the room, if you trip over the words, if you can't walk and talk at the same time, you will not book this kind of work.

If you do book this kind of work—as did Stephanie Courtney, the actress who plays Flo—it can change your life as much as a series can, in relation to money and exposure. Stephanie has been an accomplished actress for years—in theatre, episodic, film, and with The Groundlings—but now her financial life is stable, which is a gift for an actor. There is no longer a stigma to doing commercial work. Being the Mac in Apple's "Get a Mac" campaign certainly didn't hurt Justin Long's career!

Dialogue within the commercial. This type of audition is when you're doing a scene, albeit a very short one, with one or more others. The dialogue can be witty boyfriend/girlfriend banter related in some way to beer, it can be a heartfelt discussion between a mother and daughter about what cell phone coverage to choose. You have less than thirty seconds to reveal yourself within the context of the scene. You are usually auditioning with another actor or two, so you must also be a generous and equal scene partner, just as you would in a play. If you make it all about you and trying to stand out, you'll destroy the delicacy of the scene and the chemistry that absolutely needs to be created between the actors for us to be engaged in what is going on. If we think you're a show-off we won't hire you.

Subtle humor, like those found in one-camera comedies, is very common in these commercials. In fact, when I was casting commercials, the common character description and prototype we got from the client about what or who they're looking for was "Ed Helms from *The Office*" or "Aubrey Plaza from *Parks and Recreation.*" The ad executives always seem to want someone similar to whatever is the hottest comedic show on TV at the time of casting. We look for actors with an easy way with comedy, who aren't working too hard at being funny. We also look for strong improv skills because it's inevitable you will be asked to go off book and improvise the situation with your scene partner. Usually the copy is so short that we need to get a stronger sense of you and how spontaneous and loose you can be in a pinch if the scene as written isn't working. Improv weeds out the strong from the weak, so to speak.

These auditions not only involve dialogue but, more importantly, they involve actions such as brushing your teeth while your wife talks to you, or cheering at a football game while drinking a Coke. And since you're doing these activities on camera, you're confined to the space you can use. Your actions need to be focused, precise and well thought-out before you come into the audition or make your self-tape. Sometimes you can use actual props but often you can't, so not only do you have to be strong at improv, you have to be good at pantomime. Still think booking commercials is easy?

Type-wise, clients tend to choose men who are not too studly and women who are not too gorgeous—the Everyman and Everywoman, those actors with whom the consumer can best identify. I've seen clients more often than not pass on an actress because she's too pretty, presuming she will intimidate the rest of us normal folks into not buying the product. The more "normal" an actor is, the more he will work in commercials.

Non-speaking roles. These commercials where you don't speak involve you doing something while a song or voice over plays underneath. It could be a Bud commercial where a bunch of guys are having fun at a bar and checking out hot women, or it could be just you smiling, eating pie at an Applebees. Your face might go by in a nanosecond but, believe me, the clients will debate over whose is the best face to represent their product. They take nothing lightly and in fact are as hard to please as the producers and network executives who work in episodic.

As with episodic, clients look for actors who don't mug for the camera. They choose actors who make it look natural and easy. Since you're not speaking in these types of auditions, it's all about your reactions, your thoughts reflected in your face and eyes, and they hate actors who overreact. Keep it real by revealing yourself in everything you do.

In conclusion regarding commercial acting, beware of direction to be goofy or over the top. Always keep the work grounded, make it clever but not stupid, funny but not obnoxious. There is a fine line between what is endearing and what is just gross and inauthentic. That line divides getting the job from not getting it.

Oh, and don't fast forward through the commercials when you're watching episodic. They are free acting classes.

Non-Union Spots. What's changed a lot in the commercial world since my first edition of this book in 2009 is the union status of commercial spots and web-only content. More and more commercial producers have stopped making their work under the SAG-AFTRA umbrella as a way to save money. In this way, actors are left making a lot less because those lucrative SAG-AFTRA commercials are gone or, worse, are offered only to the big stars. Have you noticed how many stars are now doing the voiceovers in commercials?

This is true even in Los Angeles or New York City, where non-union commercials used to be rarely produced. Now, the majority of them are. Getting a non-union gig usually means getting a buyout in perpetuity for all media based on how often the commercial is broadcast on various media and for how long. The buyout is usually somewhere in the range of $1000-$3000, and there are no ongoing residuals And actors are accepting this, because they want to work.

4 IN PERSON AUDITIONS VS. SELF-TAPE

It's been said that *auditioning* is the actor's job, not the performance on a set or on a stage. Getting to be in a show or film—with other actors, craft services, wardrobe and makeup to make you look and feel great, a trailer (even if it's a honey wagon), and a *paycheck*—is pretty sexy.

Auditioning itself, however, is *not* sexy. It's mysterious and nerve-wracking. You are basically creating something living and breathing in a world of its own with not a lot to go on, in either an audition room or on a self-tape. If you can't audition well, you won't get the chance to be in a cool film that premieres at Sundance or get to drive onto the Paramount lot. Mastering the audition is about you being able to reveal your charisma in all its beauty within a nanosecond of entering that room or within the first 10 seconds of a self-tape.

If you can't reveal your charisma in the room or on a self-tape, you won't book the job. The writers, producers, and directors who sit in on the callbacks or watch the self-tapes that the casting director forwards to them are those parental figures you can never please. You'll never be good enough—they'll find the oddest things to fault you on (shirt is wrinkled, too much attitude, etc.)

However, when you're able to master the audition, when you're able to reveal to the casting director, producer, or director *who you really are*—your natural charisma and individual humanity in all its beautiful rawness—they'll adore you as only the best lovers can. They'll make you a star and you'll make their work (especially the writing) better than it is.

During my years as a casting director for network episodic, I had the great fortune to have worked on not just one but two Emmy® Award-winning episodic shows, *Frasier* and *Arrested Development*.

Every actor who utters even one line on any film or show you watch—all those hundreds, thousands of people who make a living as actors—had to impress a casting director. We are the keepers of the gate and we are constantly looking for exceptional actors, and, if we're lucky, the next big star to lead through that gate.

I am a fan of actors. During the eight years I worked on *Frasier* I was able to meet and work not only with the brilliant regular cast of the show —Kelsey Grammer, David Hyde Pierce, John Mahoney, Peri Gilpin, Jane Leeves, Dan Butler, Edward Hibbert and Tom McGowan—but also with a parade of incredible guest stars. These included James Earl Jones, Sir Derek Jacobi, Zooey Deschanel, Eva Marie Saint, Michael Keaton, Teri Hatcher, Virginia Madsen and Jean Smart to name just a few. Then there were the hundreds of future stars who came in to my auditions when they were as yet unknown. For some—Dakota Fanning, Jessica Alba, Eva Mendez, Sandra Oh, Chad Michael Murray and Erica Christiansen—it was one of their very first auditions. These, and thousands of good working actors, came in on a daily basis to audition for all the speaking roles on *Frasier* and the other many shows and films I worked on concurrently. I touched so many lives and helped give so many worthy actors their first big break. I was there at all the audition sessions, the table reads, the rehearsals, the shoot nights, the parties, the martinis, for many, many years.

This meant thousands upon thousands of hours spent in auditions. I am an expert on auditioning. All casting directors are. Actors do not fully understand auditioning. Directors and producers do not fully understand auditioning. I can't tell you how many actors I championed after seeing brilliant work on stage or in a small independent film only to then have them come into the audition room and tank. For some reason, they did not display the same charisma I had seen in a different context. There are a lot of frustrating hours in the audition room and watching those endless self-tapes, for those of us rooting for our favorite actors, those who have truly moved us. If the director or producer or whomever is the decision-maker in this process does not see or experience "the goods" in the audition or self-tape, they cannot be convinced otherwise. If we push our case too much, they will feel railroaded and if we do convince them, they will resent it in the long run. Casting directors do not make the final decision.

The audition process for a casting director is not only frustrating, it is boring. For a typical primetime network and cable episodic pilot, we'll see 300 actors per role. In a pilot that has six to fifteen series regulars, that means hearing the same material over and over again until we'd rather poke our eyes out than hear the same scene one more time. Sometimes the material is brilliant and sometimes, not so much, but even the most brilliant material gets old after the hundredth reading. Now multiply that by ten.

Watching literally hundreds of self-tapes for any given project is also incredibly boring and tedious. Most actors don't understand what makes a great self-tape because they haven't had to watch a million of them. Because so many come in, we literally don't have the time to watch all of them all the way through. If you don't grab us in the first 10 seconds, we are moving on.

Also know that the project, whether it's a show or a film or even a commercial, is always the number one concern—not your feelings, your time, or your career. The folks that hire you might fall in love with you, but they don't really care about you that much. Just know that going in and you won't get your heart broken.

Please don't go into the audition seeking approval. The audition is all about booking a job so you can practice your craft as an actor. The good actors share their talent with an audience. "Fulfilling your dreams" is not really why you should go into the acting profession and it certainly won't fix what ails you. Dealing with your personal issues through therapy or a spiritual journey will make you feel better, not the adoration of people you don't know.

If you're a *healthy* actor, what are the unspoken rules of an audition? These rules I refer to are not known by agents or acting coaches who have never cast; otherwise, you wouldn't hear advice like "make bold choices" or "take your time before you start the audition—it's all about you and your time." Comments like these—given to actors with all good intentions —make me nervous. They lack a basic understanding of auditioning.

The Rules of the In-Person Audition

I much prefer to run in-person auditions over watching endless self-tapes. It's much more labor intensive to organize and run these auditions, but the benefits far outweigh the downsides. First of all, the actor gets the opportunity to be directed—a strong casting director will guide your audition in such a way that it will help you book the job. Only we know the style of the particular project and what the writer-producer or director favors in an actor.

The first round of auditions are usually just with the casting director. This session is called a "pre-read." We will choose the best actors from this preliminary session to go to the "callback." In episodic television, the callback is the "producer's session" and in film, the callback is the "director's session."

So you arrive at the pre-read, sign in on a SAG-AFTRA sheet that is placed in the waiting area, and take a seat. Don't visit or talk with the other actors in the waiting area. You will be tempted, especially when you start to know and like a lot of your fellow actors, to share war stories or catch up with them on a social level. You don't want to come off as unfriendly or stuck up, right? Just be polite and refrain from visiting. Concentrate on your task at hand. Use this precious time to focus, meditate, and run through your material. Remember, *the audition is the work for the actor*. Each audition is precious and you should treat it as such, no matter how many you go on or how many years you've been doing it.

I knew a girl whose parents sacrificed a lot of time and money for her to be in Los Angeles and work as a young actress. She was quite good and was able to make an adjustment in her performance when she was focused. Her issue as an actress was that she tended to be a bit too perky for most directors' and producers' tastes. Her manager had properly coached her in preparation for an audition for a very serious scene in a studio film. However, while she was waiting to go in to the audition, she was playing with a couple of the other young actresses—talking, making up stories—basically, being an outgoing, happy ten-year-old. She was not concentrating on the scene or the emotional life of the character. When her name was called, she entered the audition a happy and perky kid, exactly what she was told by her manager *not* to be. This was a juicy role in a prestigious, serious film. Word got back to her manager that she was not focused and much too animated for the role. The manager told the agent, and then the agent was reluctant to send her in for any more roles.

It's very tough for an agent to get an audition for an unknown. The agent and manager both put their reputations and taste on the line. Once an actor blows an audition, they get put on the "too risky" list. With the time, money, and emotion spent getting in the door, you can't blow one audition. This is a serious business, not a "game." You need to be ready to do the scene as soon as your name is called to enter the audition. There is no prep or warm up once you're in there. Your prep and warm up time is in the waiting room.

Have your headshot and résumé (already stapled together) with you as you're waiting in the waiting room. Your "pic and res," as we call them, must be ready for you to hand to the casting director when requested, which is usually with the first greeting. Don't assume the casting director already has your materials in hand. Even if they do, they still need an artifact with which to remember you and to help organize the session as a whole. If they don't have a hard copy pic and res of you in the audition, you run the risk of being forgotten.

Always have a set on your person, not in your purse or briefcase. The time you take to retrieve your purse or briefcase and find these items is wasted time and wasted time is irritating to the casting director. Have it on you so you can hand it over in one simple move. Don't have your résumé separate from your headshot, in which case you or the casting director will have to take the time to get a stapler and staple them together. Irritating.

Casting directors are very impatient people. We have so many folks breathing down our necks—directors, producers, network and studio executives, agents, actors—and goodness knows what personal issues we have at any given moment. This all might seem silly, mundane, and have nothing whatsoever to do with acting or doing good work, but trust me, it makes a difference in our opinion of you. The audition location is like a factory of acting; we have to get actors in and out very quickly because we have to see a lot of folks in one session. We can't waste precious time waiting for you to get yourself together.

Honestly, sometimes we just don't have the time to be forgiving, generous, and nice when you don't have your act together. We help you out by bringing you in for the audition and giving you an opportunity to act. You can help us out by bringing your "A" game, always.

Always bring your "sides" (the material for the audition) in with you. Casting directors get nervous when we see you without your sides. We either think, "damn it, they didn't get their sides and they aren't prepared," or "damn it, this cocky actor thinks he's so memorized, he doesn't need his sides anymore."

You do not get points for memorizing. Remember, it's an audition not a performance. You can refer back to your sides if you need to during the actual reading. The main thing is to keep the audition moving. It's worse to "go up" (forget your lines) than it is to look down at your sides for the next line. When you go up you get disconnected from the character and the person you're reading with. When you have to look down, you can do so quickly and keep the scene flowing. That being said, there is an art to using your sides, because a great audition is one in which you are connected to the reader. If you are looking down too much, you also disconnect from the other person and the chemistry of the scene will be lost.

So you enter the audition, all ready to go with your sides and headshot and résumé. Either the casting director greets you at the door, or you're brought in by the assistant or associate and introduced to the casting director. Don't put your hand out to shake the casting director's hand unless he or she extends their hand first. Let the casting director guide you on manners. Some casting directors have issues with germs because we see a lot of people in one day. If we have eight hours of auditions in a single day, we might see 200 plus actors that day. If we shake every person's hand, that's a hell of a lot of germs. We come in contact with more human bodies than even a school teacher, perhaps as much as politicians on the campaign trail. We're not necessarily paranoid (although some of us might be) but we're practical. Plus, it's an audition, not a job interview, therefore, no handshaking unless the casting director initiates it.

Don't come in and want to chat before the actual reading begins. Again, let the casting director be your guide in the manners of their audition room. If we want to chat with you then you can chat. Maybe we'll ask you about something on your résumé or mention a play we just saw you in. Don't come into the audition and gush about the show, the drive over to the audition, or us. This is extraneous and sucks up precious time. Just come in as the most natural "you" possible, say "Hi," and be ready to sit or stand in place and begin.

This early in the audition, before it's even really started, the casting director has already decided whether he or she likes you or not. Most auditioners are assessed through the eyes and by the way you walk, stand, and sit. Are your eyes clear and alive? Or are they murky and full of fear and uncertainty? Are you stiff, physically? Are you relaxed with a natural posture? Do we feel comfortable being around you? It is your job to make us comfortable, not the other way around. We must sense that you can handle yourself in any situation, especially on a set, which can be chaotic with a lot of insecure people running around counting on you, the actor, to know what you're doing. You must reflect a reassuring confidence the moment you enter and take your place.

Please don't ask the following questions of the casting director:

- "What are you looking for?"

- "What are you not finding in the other actors?"

- "Should I be natural or more 'charactery?'"

- "I prepared three versions. Which one would you like me to do first?"

- "What is my relationship to the lead actor?"

These might be fine questions in a different context, like at a job interview or in a play rehearsal, but not in the audition. These questions reek of "actor" (and not in a good way). We don't want to see the wheels turning; we don't want to see you working. We want you to come into the

63

audition focused and owning the space, not needy or insecure, not a deer in headlights. What are we looking for? We are always looking for "you" in the scene and for you to be brilliant and interesting.

Whatever questions you might have can be answered ahead of time by either the "breakdown" (brief description of the project and the characters) or from information you glean directly from the dialogue and action in the scene. Sometimes, concocting an elaborate "backstory" (the character's history) that's not found directly in the script—adding an incest twist where there is none or making the character an exchange student from Germany—can ruin the audition.

Sometimes a casting director will ask you if you have any questions, as it's just a good neutral icebreaker to get the process rolling. The best answer to that question is "No."

Don't ever say, "I just got these sides." Even if that's true and your audition is suffering because of it, never say this. It makes everyone look bad—you, your agent (for getting you the sides late), and the casting director (for getting the sides to the agent late). There are never any excuses for being underprepared. And if there are somewhat legitimate reasons, we don't want to hear them.

One of the elements that has really changed from when I began in the '90s, is that all casting directors are "putting actors on tape" for the pre-read. In all the years I worked on sitcoms, we never used a video camera in the audition. Now, you can't be a casting director without one. Who could have predicted back in the day that the casting director would need to have the skills of a filmmaker?

Audition tapings are not done in ideal circumstances. We don't shoot you on a set with hair, make-up and professional quality lighting provided. We are not capturing you with the Red One digital camera. The technology we often use is very simple so as to be cost effective. Because the footage we take is raw, it's even more crucial than ever that your auditions stand out.

The presence of the camera in audition changes the dynamic of the interaction between actor and casting director. It makes it harder for an actor to emotionally connect with the material and with the reader. Sometimes you have to stand a certain way in front of a wall or screen, which might feel awkward and make you self-conscious. Questions might float in your mind like "where do I look? At the reader or directly into the camera?" This will of course avert your concentration from the task at hand, which is to be attractive and draw us in. What's an actor to do?

We tape all the pre-reads and then assess whose auditions we're going to forward to the client. Producers, directors, and ad agency clients alike prefer watching auditions remotely, from their device of choice, in their own time. The new technology has been a boon for these busy people, who used to have to sit through four to six hours of live auditions, taking time away from their already hectic schedules.

Some clients like to watch all of the auditioners. In one day—for a commercial for instance—we might see 120 actors. I doubt the client who wants to watch all of the actors we brought in is going to watch all 120 auditions. For those clients who just want to see the best, the casting office will upload and forward only a selection.

The actual audition begins.... Most of the time, you will be reading with the casting director (although sometimes there is a "reader" so the casting director can just sit back and watch), and the first thing you should do is connect with the reader/casting director in every way you can. What you don't want to do is heedlessly begin, barreling through the material. You don't want to just read the lines and, conversely, you don't want to—heaven forbid—overact. Relax and make great eye contact, revealing right off the bat your charisma. You must fall in love with the person you're doing the scene with. Just look in their eyes and find their humanity. Not an easy task, especially if the casting director is looking down at her sides, glancing at your résumé, or appearing irritated, tired or both. Don't get sucked into our energy! Make us get sucked into yours. Make your two eyes laser beams and bore into the casting director's eyes. I'm not saying make your eyes unnaturally big and look at us like an adoring fan, I'm just saying connect human to human. Make it about us, just as with any scene, whether it is in a film, on episodic, or in a play. It's not about you or how you're doing, it's about the other person.

The hard fact is that you will hardly ever do an audition with another actor, especially not in episodic. You have got to learn to make it work with the non-actor before you. With film auditions, if you get a callback, you will probably have a "chemistry read" to assess the connection you have with another actor, but only if you're up for the lead. If your scene is with Brad Pitt and you're a day player, then no, Brad will not be doing a chemistry read with you. With pilot auditions, if you're up for a leading part, you might—if you're really lucky—get to do your final audition for network with another actor. This means that you and an actor up for the lead opposite you audition in front of the network executives who are producing the show. But if you're auditioning for a supporting role, you're on your own—you might not meet all your fellow actors on a project until the first rehearsal when cast, crew, director, creators, and producers gather for a "table read" (the first read through of the script once all the roles are cast). All the more reason for you to find chemistry with the casting director any way you can. We are all you have at this point in the casting process.

If you drop the momentum of the scene by going up or botching a word or a line, try to keep going as if nothing were wrong. If the casting director wants to stop you at this point, she will, but, if not, just keep going.

66

The best auditions are smooth and easy. You have a strong connection, make good eye contact, and you keep it moving. If you're present in the moment, revealing your true self, and you don't need to correct yourself or start over, you will make the casting director very happy. If you absolutely must start over, it's imperative that you do a brilliant job the second time around. Once you have messed up, you have gotten yourself into a hole, and it is difficult to climb out of it entirely. Don't dig yourself in deeper by messing up yet again and apologizing too much. You might salvage the audition if you're flawless the second go-round, but even then you're on shaky ground.

Remember, there is no real rehearsal time on the set and we have to feel confident that we can send you to the stage.

They way you deliver the lines should seem like a real conversation with the other person. Nothing more, nothing less.

The more you're prepared with the material, the more relaxed you will be. The more relaxed you are, the more you'll be able to have good eye contact and connect with us. We're just looking for a connection. We're looking for your humanity within the context of the scene, not your acting.

When the reading is done, the casting director will say something like "That's it. Thank you so much." They also might say "excellent," or "that's all you have to do," or "very nice." This is all meaningless. Not to say that it's empty praise, but this is not feedback on which to hang your hat. If you get a callback, then you did very well. If you don't get a callback, then you didn't impress us. Most of the time, that's all the feedback you will get. There just isn't time for the casting director to critique every actor.

I give very direct feedback to actors I know on a personal basis or to those whom I want to help out if there's time, but *it's not our job in the audition to teach you to be a better actor.* Our job is to find good actors for the shows and films we work on. We are beholden to the people who hire us. We love actors, but we simply don't have the time to give you everything. Don't let that make you bitter toward us.

If you go on a lot of auditions and don't get called back, don't convince yourself "they're just not looking for my type." The fault might lie with you. Don't expect us to answer the question that will live eternally at the back of your mind, no matter how confident, trained and experienced you are. "Do I have what it takes to make it as an actor?" We will never tell you point blank "that sucks," or "you should give up being an actor right now," or "you have absolutely no sex appeal whatsoever." We won't tell you. We can't tell you. We don't have the insight and power for that. I've seen incredibly weak actors, whom I thought didn't have a prayer, learn from their bad auditions, improve over time, and end up working a lot. I've seen actors perform brilliantly in either a play or a film, but then tank in an audition. As long as you're willing to get help where you need it, outside of the audition, then you will eventually master it.

Your audition is over and the casting director says, "Thank you very much." Don't, under any circumstance, continue the audition by saying, "Would you like to see it another way?" or "I can be directed." You're showing your desperate actor side by saying anything other than "thank you." If we want to see it another way, we'll ask for it. We know you can be directed, you're an actor for goodness sake! Simply leave. Don't sulk out defeated or storm out angry, just graciously exit.

Once you leave the audition, forget about it. Don't brood over it, don't relive it over and over in your distraught mind, and don't try to figure out how you could have done it differently or better. Forget about it! Effortlessly move on to the next task at hand.

Never get in your car, drive away, think about a new way to do the scene, then drive back to the audition room and ask to do it again. I've had this happen many times, and it's just embarrassing and uncomfortable. If the casting director wants to be nice by agreeing to let you do it again, you're now in a hole you can never climb out of because it's massive. You'll waste everyone's time. Just leave it alone at the first "thank you very much."

Making a Strong Self-Tape

Self-tape is now the most popular type of audition process. This has been one of the big changes since this book's previous edition, and it's the one that bothers me the most. I don't know how a casting director—or a writer-producer and director for that matter—can hire an actor just off self-tape without having had the experience with them in person, especially not knowing how many takes it took the actor to get that strong audition.

How is an actor to know how to play the scene without *some* guidance from the casting director actually casting the project? Sure, if you go to a taping service, you might get some coaching, but it's not from a casting director, which honestly, makes all the difference in the world. Going to a taping service costs the actor money, which is really bothersome to me. And if an actor has the right set up at home (or on the road), they also have to have the skills to download, edit, and upload their auditions on a computer or device to either get it in Breakdown Services' Eco-Cast (more on this service later in the book) or via DropBox or WeTransfer, depending on what the casting director prefers. This also means you have to have the most up-to-date technology and equipment and have a mastery of all the technical elements—otherwise you will drive yourself crazy.

I've heard actors say that self-tapes are a godsend because you don't have to drive around town so much going to auditions and that if you don't live in an area where big production is taking place, you can still have acting opportunities. I think with that convenience comes what I call the "black hole of self-tapes." An actor sends his or her self-tape audition to the casting director (or their agent forwards the file) and will never ever get feedback on that audition unless (1) you get a callback, (2) you book the job, (3) the casting director knows you very well and, because you are very, very close to being what the director is looking for, requests a re-do with some notes—an occurrence that is considerably rare.

Without feedback, how are you supposed to know how to improve your self-tapes if you aren't booking?

I've watched *a lot* of self-tapes. Most are not strong. I've been doing workshops on self-taping. When we, as a group, watch all the self-tapes that the participants have sent ahead of time, everyone is shocked how little they know of what makes a great self-tape and despondent to know that most of the self-tapes are not strong enough to send off to the writer-producer or director of this pretend job. These workshops are always an eye-opening experience.

Here are the basic precepts we discuss in the workshop:

1) **If you don't grab us in the first 10 seconds, we won't watch the whole tape;** in fact, it is highly likely we'll turn it off right at the 10-second mark. We get hundreds and hundreds of self-tapes for every role in every project. We simply do not have the time to watch all of them all the way through. We are good at what we do —we can tell within 10 seconds whether you are emotionally compelling or not. We can tell if you are focused, quietly confident, and present in the moment. We can tell whether you are giving us a character that is a fully realized human being and not a stick figure.

70

You can't play one-note in a self-tape. You have to still reveal your authentic charisma just as you do in an audition room... probably even more so—we can't coax it out of you, after all, because we aren't in the room where you are doing the self-tape.

Since you only have 10 seconds to grab us, don't waste the very first moment by trying to play an action or looking down at an imaginary prop. We need to see your eyes right way, and you either need to be saying a line or reacting to the line that your reader is saying. Don't walk into the scene, even if the action says "he enters." Just be there already. We need to see and feel you from the first nanosecond. If there's a lot of action going on, like a fight scene, pare it down to the bare minimum. Keep it simple. We just want *you*. We don't care if you can mime well. We care if your acting is emotionally compelling.

2) **Keep the framing to a close-up—from the chest or shoulders up.** Eyes need to be the focus.

3) **Your Eyeline should be straight ahead, looking at the reader**. The reader should be just left of the camera, close enough to touch it. Don't make the eyeline up or down, just level with you. Yes, even if the other character is supposed to be standing above you or taller or you are towering over them. If you are talking to several different characters, keep it simple. One character you look at the reader, the other character, just off to the other side of the camera. Same eyeline (the reader, of course, stays in one place even if reading for many different roles). Never ever lean over. Not only will you go out of frame, but your eyes will no longer be the focus. Plus, it just looks strange.

4) **Ignore the Character Description** I know, I know, this is an odd thing to say. I'm sure script writers will want to lambaste me for this

thinking, but trust me: it works, especially for the co-star roles when there is very little to go on. Your brief character description might read "cranky cop" or "waitress with attitude," but, as was discussed earlier, you can't play one note. If you play the role "cranky," you will be one note and not a fully dimensional character. You will be boring or too big. But if, instead, you simply put *yourself* in the situation as depicted, and find your five different emotions, one of which could be cranky or irritated, you will have a dynamic audition. You were *chosen* to audition out of the hundreds of actors submitted. You must be right for the role in some way. That's all you need to know. They want *you* in this role. Give them what they want. Believe me, you are enough.

5) **Have the right equipment without spending a fortune.**

- **Lighting:** Photography Photo Portrait Studio 600W Day Light Umbrella Continuous Lighting Kit by LimoStudio (product number LMS103) for around $50.00

- **iPhone:** What other camera can compete with the 1080 or 4K camera on these smartphones that won't cost a fortune? Plus, the internal mic is so great, you don't need an external mic, which can sometimes emit a buzzing sound when you play it back. (DO NOT use the camera on your computer!) If you instead want to use a Canon or any other brand, that's fine, too.

- **Tripod:** I've been using a cheap Vivitar VPT3662 62-Inch Tripod for years that costs under $30. No need to get a more expensive, fancy one (unless you are using an expensive, fancy camera.)

- **Tripod Mount:** I use a mount I found on **caddybuddy.com** for $24.00. Been using this for years. Works great.

- **Solid Background:** I personally don't like the blue or grey background that is required sometimes on self-tapes. I don't think it enhances the face and eyes of an actor. Plus, in order to get a blue or grey solid background, you have to buy a freestanding backdrop stand (yet another piece of equipment) or worse, hang a blue or grey sheet on the wall, which will inevitably have ripples, wrinkles, or lines, making it look amateurish. Even worse, you could use a "green screen" which would just be terrible. I prefer a white wall background—find a spot in your apartment or house where you can move the furniture and/or take whatever is on the wall down with ease. Simple. No expenditure.

6) **Have a real, live reader**. Find an acting buddy (or several)…. Enlist a family member…. Do whatever is necessary to avoid using an electronic voice. From a casting director's perspective, hearing an electronic voice is distracting and sounds just plain strange. Also, you can't connect with an electronic voice. And if you don't connect with the other person in a scene, your dialogue will just feel like you are saying lines instead of having a conversation.

7) **Editing and Uploading/Sending Off.** As you can probably tell by now, I'm all about Apple products and think they are the easiest to use for actors and filmmakers. You can edit and upload to Actors Access or send via Dropbox or WeTransfer directly from your iPhone. iMovie is free on Apple products, and there's nothing easier to use than that. Or you can Airdrop your raw footage from your iPhone to your Mac and edit and send it off that way.

8) **Go to a taping service** if you just don't want to mess with items 5–7 above. Taping service costs range from $1 a minute to $80 an hour, depending on how much coaching you want. If you are auditioning a lot, this can cost a fortune, which is why I've gone through the steps and equipment needed to do it yourself.

9) **Slating.** Slating can be awkward and most slates I watch don't reveal the true person who is stating their name, height, role, and if they are "local hire" or not. Slates are necessary, however, so do them right. Say your information as if you were talking to a close friend. Reveal who you are. Don't sound "professional" as if you were at a stiff job interview. Be real, natural, not trying to be too funny or too cutesy or too serious. Just connect with that camera as if it were a friend. Keep it simple. Always put the slate either at the end of your self-tape or in a separate file, depending on the directions provided by the casting director. If it's not stated on the breakdown, then put it at the end of the audition, to be on the safe side. Never start the audition with a slate, unless of course it's requested.

If you have not been requested to go on tape by either the casting director (directly) or the agent who is submitting you, then you're sending a "blind submission." Blind submissions can be a waste of time. I know some actors read something online—like that so-and-so casting director is looking for the next action star in Ryan Cooglar's next film. The actor then takes the time, money and energy to find the contact information of the casting director online, create an audition tape, and forward the audition to the unsuspecting casting director. The odds of that audition being watched are a million to one. We simply don't have the time to view auditions unless they were requested by us or forwarded by an agent we trust. And the odds of that blind submission being good enough to warrant a callback are even more astronomical. If someone can prove me wrong by booking a huge job on a blind submission, please let me know and I will stand corrected.

74

Callbacks

When you get a callback, congratulations! This is no small feat. For one normal episodic co-star or guest star role, we'll most likely pre-read twenty to fifty actors and only bring five to the producers' callback. We're usually casting six to eight roles per episode for a half-hour comedy and twenty per episode for an hour show, so you do the math; we're seeing a lot of actors in a short time frame. Getting a callback is second only to actually booking the job, and you should be ecstatic to make it to that round. You have our attention. We love you. We only bring the top auditioners to the callback as our jobs depend on the acting ability of the actors we choose.

Some actors are considered "straight to producers." They are in this category because we know them so well and are 100% confident in their ability to audition well. Oftentimes, these actors will have booked with us before or have excelled at their pre-reads. Another reason an actor may bypass the pre-read process is if a particular actor's agent insists their client doesn't pre-read. It's a prestige factor. The actor has worked consistently and so why should they have to meet with the casting director first? This happens a lot during pilot season. I understand this way of thinking—auditions of any kind are a chore and isn't it nice to go directly to the callback without the preliminary audition?

Skipping the pre-read is not always in the actor's best interest, however. More often than not, as I mentioned earlier, the only direction an actor will get is with the casting director. We know what the producers are looking for and it is only during the pre-read that we have the time and inclination to direct the actor to help them book the job. The callback for episodic is always very stressful and not the best time for direction to take place. The producers are incredibly busy folks and the casting session takes them away from the writers' room. The producers, even the sweet ones, can't wait for the casting session to be over so they can resume writing. Also, some are uncomfortable in the audition as they might not know how to talk to an actor.

According to Phil Rosenthal *(Everybody Loves Raymond* creator), the truth of the matter is "a television writer's main preoccupation is 'where's lunch? Where are we going to order from today because we have a lot of work to do, so we're going to work through lunch.' Lunch is the only sunshine coming into the room." Since they do not wake up in the morning looking forward to hearing actors speak their words for the very first time in the callback audition room, it's best to meet with the casting director alone first before entering.

It is during the callback for episodic that an actor really needs to nail the audition on the first take. If you've gotten a callback from a pre-read, it's imperative you recreate the final audition you had in the pre-read session, the exact audition that got you the callback in the first place. Don't go home between your pre-read and your callback and think, "Oh, how about if I add this cute line reading. I can make it funnier that way!" If your callback is substantially different from your pre-read, you'll irritate the casting director, which you want to avoid. We're helping you out. We took the time to direct you in the first place. Don't mess with a good thing. We know what we're doing, and even if some of us don't, listen to us anyway.

This is an extreme case, but I once had an actor come in to a producer's session. I had pre-read and directed him. He was difficult in the audition but a good actor who I had seen in plays at the Mark Taper Forum in Los Angeles. I wanted to give him a shot even though he was fighting me in the pre-read. He came into the callback and had the gall to say to the producers, "I don't agree with the direction I was given by the casting director and so I'd like to try it my own way." The actor not only embarrassed me in front of my boss, but he came off as difficult and argumentative, two traits not highly regarded in actors.

As always, be a perfect human being in the callback. Be brilliant and keep the casting director happy.

The callback for film, which is with the director and not the producer, is considerably less stressful than for episodic. You're meeting with the director so you will be directed, which is a gift. For episodic, you're auditioning for the next episode while the producers are shooting the current one. This situation is very distracting for them. The atmosphere is frenetic. For film, it's only about that particular movie, and so the pace is leisurely in comparison. Unless you're auditioning for a series regular, the producers in episodic don't have time to get to know you as a person separate from your audition. In film, the director wants to get to know you. He will chat with you before the audition begins. He might ask you questions about the role. He might tell you that you can veer from the script and improvise if you feel inclined. This will hardly ever happen in episodic unless it's for an improvised show.

No matter what room you're in, whether it's for episodic episodic or a studio film, go with the flow of the room and let the casting director be your guide.

You will book the job if and only if the producer or the director is excited by you and if you're a great fit for the role. You don't have to be what they initially imagined for the role. You don't have to fit the character description in either the breakdown or the script, you just have to fit the role in the callback. You have to own that role. The actor who will book a particular role is so committed to that part that he's not going to let anyone else have it, or so it seems. There is energy, passion, and a sense of spontaneity to the audition. The actor has abandoned himself to the role. There is no self-consciousness to the audition. We, the casting director and either the producer or director, just sit back and enjoy. There is a depth, command, and sense of either joy or sadness, depending on the genre, to the audition.

As with the pre-reads, you will be videotaped during the callback. Thanks to the new technology, it's so easy for, let's say, the Director of Casting at CBS to watch the auditions online. Whereas previously we might have faxed over the headshot and résumé of the actor we wanted to hire for a guest spot, it's now the standard for the networks and studios to approve of nearly every role that is cast on an episodic by watching the digital uploads.

The same is true with films, commercials, even web series. The "client"—such as Nike or Subway (both of which I've worked for on web series)—must always approve of an actor before we can hire him or her. By "client" I mean a whole team of people that includes the head of marketing, the creatives, and even the CEO in some cases. The folks in positions of power must watch the auditions, and thanks to the new technology, they don't have to travel around the country anymore to do so.

5 HOW DO WE CHOOSE WHO GETS TO AUDITION?

Just as a writer begins with a blank page and proceeds to express his thoughts and ideas in his writing, casting directors begin with a blank "Idea List," expressing ourselves in the actors we select to consider for each new casting job. Choosing which actors to give an audition slot (whether in person or self-tape) or offer a part to directly is a complicated process and requires the sensitivity and insight of a poet. I have a script in front of me—could be a classic play such as *Romeo and Juliet*, an episode from a network episodic show such as *Arrested Development,* or a cute commercial for Honda—and I have hundreds if not thousands of actors to choose from for the roles I need to cast. Who will I choose?

I bring in actors I already have a connection with and I audition actors who are new to me, submitted by an agent and/or manager via Breakdown Services or through Actors Access (an online service run by Breakdown Services through which actors with no representation can self-submit).

The actors I already have a connection with come into my sphere from so many different resources. I watch episodic, I see films and I sniff out cool web series online. I take note of the actors I think are good in all these mediums and jot their names down. I see a lot of improv shows and stand-up. I lead workshops and keep the headshots of the actors who have impressed me with their natural charisma and ease. I see a lot of theater and have bins and bins of *Playbills* and other programs from plays with little stars or hearts next to the name and headshot of the actor who moved me. I follow actors I love on Instagram and Twitter. I'm "friends" with actors I admire on Facebook.

I become a "fan," in a way, of an actor, and they become part of my arsenal, a name on one of my many lists. Casting directors are master list makers and refer back to them often. I print out cast lists via IMDb (Internet Movie Database) from movies I see and highlight the actors who stood out for me. I've created and continually update lists with such titles as "Actors I Love," "British Actors in the U.S." and "Hot Guys Under 30." I have cast lists in hundreds of notebooks from all the projects I've ever worked on. I have kept all of my audition sessions, covered in scribbled notes, since I was first allowed the privilege of being in the audition room as an intern, and I refer to these lists still. That's a heck of a lot of paper—and a ton of actors.

What's happening now, because of technology, is that casting directors can easily create and maintain an electronic database of every actor they ever cast, so they can easily find, say, "black actors under 40" by merely typing in those words or checking off boxes and searching.

So how can an actor get selected for an audition if I don't know them? You'd think with all the hundreds if not thousands of actors I already know at my fingertips, why would I ever venture outside of my own lists? It's a lot of extra work to meet new actors, and I'm already stressed as it is.

In truth, I'm always looking for actors I don't already know, and on most big jobs I work on, I turn to Breakdown Services. As described on their website, "Breakdown Services, Ltd. is the communications network and casting system that provides the most professional means to reach talent agents as well as actors when casting a project. Breakdown Services has offices in Los Angeles, New York and Vancouver and maintains affiliate relationships with sister companies in Toronto, London and Sydney. With clients in most regions of the USA and Provinces of Canada our reach extends throughout North America." That's a lot of territory and a lot of actors and agents! I know when I send out a breakdown, the floodgates will open and I'll be inundated with casting ideas.

Breakdown Services was created by Gary Marsh in 1971 and has had a monopoly on getting information from casting directors to agents and talent since then. Through their Eco Cast service, they now also provide an avenue for the casting directors to receive submissions from agents and talent electronically, which makes our lives so much easier—no more envelopes to retrieve and open.

There are two other services with which some agents require an actor to have an account, besides the ubiquitous Breakdown Services/Actors Access. Casting Networks (owned by Fox, but with the Disney takeover, its future is uncertain) and Casting Frontier are used primarily for commercials. I personally only use Breakdown Services. Breakdown Services has the *most* actors, agencies, and management companies subscribers.

My process with Breakdown Services is the following:

I read the script I've been given to work on. It could be a pilot script, a single episode of a series, a commercial, a USC student film or a web series—all of which I've worked on.

I then compose the breakdown, which is comprised of the following:

- Name of project

- Format (multi-camera sitcom, web series, short film etc.)

- Network and studio attached, if for an episodic show

- Production company name, if for a film

- Client name, if for a commercial or industrial

- Casting director name (along with associates and assistants, if any)

82

- Director name

- Writer name

- Producer(s) name(s)

- Shoot dates

- Casting session dates

- Pay rate

- Contract—SAG-AFTRA or non-union.

- Project description—story synopsis, project history and goals etc.

- Casting summary—general scope of the talent being sought (types, ages etc.)

- Role breakdown—brief description of every role available, including age range, demographic, personality, backstory, relationship to other characters etc.

I always include a statement that reads "PLEASE NO PHONE CALLS" and I never, ever include my personal email within the breakdown. Inevitably, however, agents and managers will call me and email me directly. Direct submissions are annoying. I just don't have the time to go through every single one. And I will ignore submissions emailed to me from actors I don't know.

I can choose to get submissions from Los Angeles agents and managers only, Los Angeles and New York both, or all over the country. Since I'm currently in Atlanta, I would choose Southeast only. I can also choose to get Actors Access submissions. When I am brave enough to choose this option—and most of you reading this will want me to do so

—I will need to brace myself for the onslaught. I will get headshots, résumés, and demo reels from everyone under the sun—actors who have just started acting, actors from all over the country, actors who will submit school photos. I have found fresh talent this way, but this process is incredibly time-consuming and not efficient for jobs with a quick turn-around, such as a commercial or TV episode.

The majority of the projects that you would most desire to get called in for—episodic TV, cable series, streaming services that produce high-end content (Netflix, Hulu) will not be posted on Actors Access. For the most part, the breakdowns for these projects go only to agents and managers via Breakdown Services.

Once my breakdown is complete, I take a breath and press "send." The wonderful folks in the writer's room at Breakdown Services will then format my breakdown and publish it online. Within ten minutes, I will start getting electronic submissions in my private, password-protected Breakdown Express account. Within two hours, I could have up to 1500 of them (!), grouped by role—this is not an exaggeration.

Each submission consists of a thumbnail of a headshot above a row of icons I can click on to bring up a résumé, some additional pictures, and a demo reel. Under the icons can be found the agency or management company who submitted the actor. There also might be a simple note attached, such as "classically trained" or "member of the Groundlings."

The way I go through them is down-and-dirty, because of the sheer volume. I'll look at a page of headshots—which is usually four columns of 25 rows—scanning for type, age, look and general feel. Is it a good professional headshot? Are the eyes compelling? Am I attracted to this person? And since headshots are no longer 8" x 10" printed photos, but, rather, mere thumbnail images on a screen, it really needs to be spectacular.

When I come across an actor I already know and they are right for the part, I will choose him or her first.

If I find the headshot of an actor I don't know compelling, I will then look at the résumé. I look at credits, of course, but also training. Does this person have a degree in theatre? Have they only taken random workshops or does their training reflect a commitment to the craft? If I'm casting a comedy, I'll take note of their improv, sketch and/or stand-up experience and won't bring them in unless they have some.

By scanning through the headshots and résumés as quickly as I can— so I can get through all 1500—the only thing I have to guide me is my gut. Yes, I might overlook some great people, but there is always enough to choose from and I've been casting long enough that I always find what I need with this process.

I narrow down my choices to a more manageable number of actors (from the 1500 down to, say a couple hundred). I then watch as many demo reels as I have time for from this group. The way in which casting directors can now watch demo reels is a huge positive change from the '90s when we had to watch either a physical VHS tape or a DVD. Now, with the demo reels attached to the submission via a link, I'm much more likely to watch a reel than ever before. Plus, the convenience of being able to watch it from any device anywhere in the world is a godsend.

If the demo reel doesn't grab my attention within the first 10 seconds, I will pass on the actor. If I can't determine your essence, if you're not revealing yourself in an interesting way, I won't bring you in.

A positive upshot of new technology is that demo reels no longer have to be composed solely of scenes from episodic shows that have aired or films that have played in a movie theatre. Now you can get together with some friends and create a web series. You can write, produce, and direct a

85

short film that showcases your talent, and you can do so relatively cheaply. It doesn't have to be "professional," but it absolutely must be compelling. If you're not proud of the work, don't put it up on YouTube. It could hurt you rather than help.

I've watched thousands of demo reels. The majority of demo reels from actors who have been acting for less than five years are pretty bad. Make sure the demo reel favors *you* in the scenes. We don't need to have context for the scenes and we're not interested in the other actors. Start the demo with a close up on you, if you can. Again, you've got the 10-second rule, and if you waste your precious 10 seconds showcasing the work of another actor, you've blown it. Make sure the footage you use looks like you *now*. We don't want to be taken by surprise (or worse, disappointed when you walk into the room or send us a self-tape. **A demo should not be more than one minute in length.** Believe me, when we are watching this many, we will not watch a demo any longer than that and we probably won't even watch more than 30 seconds. We see what we need to see very quickly. Make sure your best scene starts the demo.

So if your headshot, résumé and demo reel all combined manage to emotionally move me to think "I like this actor a lot," you move into the select group of actors I will bring in for an audition or from whom I will request a self-tape. By this time, I've narrowed the pool down to about 20–30 actors per role.

Breakdown Services allows you to divide this select group into "1s," "2s," or "3s" with a simple click. This is a much better and more efficient system than in the past when I had to physically place headshots in piles on my desk.

For my first session, I might just bring in the 1s, saving my 2s and 3s for backup if I don't find what I need in the first sessions. Or I might bring in 1s and 2s, saving the 3s if all else fails.

Most likely my first pre-reads will be in four-hour increments, which is about the longest any casting session can be before intense fatigue and boredom set in. Two to three hours is really best but we try to see as many actors as possible.

Typically, we schedule one person every five minutes or two every fifteen minutes. If we're seeing actors in groups—as is common with commercials—we'll schedule one group every ten minutes. If the roles are substantial (e.g. pilots) we'll schedule in longer increments of time, but not much more. At that rate, we're only seeing twelve actors an hour if we speed through. That's 48 in four hours...out of 1500. Ugh, the numbers!

Yes, there is a lot of competition. I'm not telling you anything you don't know. But, in reality, all of that competition is not brilliant. Maybe 2% of any given casting session goes really well. When you get a precious audition, be brilliant.

The difficult issue with us is that we have to wade through so many submissions. In truth, about 50%–75% of those submissions have no business being there, but we don't really know that until we get them in either in the audition room or watch their self-tape. It's really a numbers game, but the bottom line is, talent will always rise to the top, if you can hang in there.

It's not just about submitting your headshot and waiting for the Cmail (Breakdown Services' proprietary messaging app) to arrive or your agent (if you are lucky to have one) submitting you and you just sitting around eating bonbons waiting for him or her to email you. In reality, you have to still do as much leg work as if you didn't have an agent.

By leg work, I mean getting out there—physically—so we can see you and get a strong sense of the person you are and the talent you have. You have to be in plays, do stand-up, or create your own content. You have to take classes and get referrals through those teachers and students. You have to network, but in a good way. Not the slick I'm-here-to-answer-all-your-prayers way, but in the I'd-like-to-share-who-I-am-with-you kind of way. A kind of mutual networking where we get to know each other.

6 WHERE TO LIVE

New York City-Los Angeles-Atlanta

In the previous two editions of this book, I unequivocally stated "New York and Los Angeles are the only cities in which one can make a living as a full-time actor." This is no longer true. Actors now have a third very viable option—Atlanta, Georgia. Other cities where studio films and prestige episodics shoot are Chicago, Albuquerque, and New Orleans. But Atlanta is solidly in the top three locations for professional acting jobs in the country. If you could see the breakdowns sent out by casting directors, you would see that Atlanta now surpasses Los Angeles for location shooting. Canada is still a viable location for film and episodic shoots, but unless you are a star, it's nearly impossible for an American actor to get booked.

I came to Atlanta in 2016, to work as a casting director on a film. The film never got made but I stayed. I was born in Hollywood, grew up in and around all parts of Los Angeles. I'm one of the few real natives. I never in my wildest dreams thought I would relocate to the South, but I have and I love it.

It's true, most auditions now are self-tapes, and in a perfect world, it wouldn't matter where you lived in the country. But it does matter. Even though auditions aren't in person as much as they used to be, I strongly believe you still need to be part of a community that is location-based and not virtual. You need to perform on stages, whether it's in a play, doing stand-up, or part of an improv show. You need to be out there *doing* where we can find you. You need to network in a real space. You need to have like-minded artists around you for inspiration and collaboration. You need to share information with others like you so you can avoid mistakes and missteps. You need to support other artists by going to see their work.

Community is very important to any artist, but especially actors. You *need* other people *in person*. You can't act in a vacuum after all.

Credits from smaller markets don't mean anything in Los Angeles, New York, and even now Atlanta unless you're doing leads at a regional theatre. To some producers and casting directors, even those prestigious credits don't have weight. So if you want and need to relocate, you'd better just do it, and the sooner the better. Time is not on your side. Relocating is not a cheap endeavor, so choose wisely and what's right for you.

Choosing which city is best for you might be decided based on your financial situation. It costs a lot of money to be an actor. Truth is, it costs a lot of money to be anything in the arts. I had to take out a loan for my first year in casting. The income I received while paying my dues was at the poverty level.

Actors have a lot of expenses right from the get-go. You really can't skimp on any of them.

Typical expenses are:
- Transportation (bus, car, gas, maintenance, insurance)
- Housing (rent, utilities)
- Cable or streaming services (you *must* watch lots of films and episodic television)
- Tickets for concerts, plays, and films
- Headshots
- Smartphone/Camera
- Self-tape services
- Coaching sessions
- Computer
- Classes/Workshops
- Subscriptions to IMDB Pro, Breakdown Services/Actors Access, and Casting Networks
- Office Supplies
- Clothes
- Grooming
- Therapy

- Socializing
- Airfare
- Healthcare

- Gift-giving
- SAG-AFTRA Dues

Los Angeles (and really all of Southern California) has become exorbitantly expensive and is frankly giving New York City a run for it's money. *Everything* is expensive, from rents ($1400 low end for a studio, if you are lucky) to food costs to gasoline to honestly most everything listed above as expenses. If you are not a wealthy person nor come from a wealthy family, you will most likely be sharing a living space with at least three people. It pains me to say because I defended Los Angeles for years —it's difficult for someone with an average income to afford to live there. As an actor, you are also going to have to create your own content, which often costs money. This will be difficult to do in Los Angeles without the help of a really good support system—a mate, wife, husband, partner, parent, pal—people who can fully support you emotionally and financially. Ideally, you will find people who are not only deeply committed to you in this endeavor but is also an emotionally solid as persons in their own right. If they are jealous, they will not hang in there during the inevitable times when you'll be hanging out with very successful, attractive people.

Los Angeles is the place to go if you want to pursue comedy. Upright Citizens Brigade and The Groundlings are the epicenter of comedy in the country. More episodic comedy shows (especially multi-cams) are created and shot here than anywhere else—yes, even Atlanta.

Actors over 30 who want to relocate to Los Angeles have a tough road ahead. Unless you're a character actor who actually becomes more marketable as you get older, the difficulty of "getting in the door" becomes exponentially harder the older you get. I'm not saying it's impossible, I'm saying the already high odds are even higher. The cost might become greater as one has to sacrifice family, relationships, and a steady job. I don't want to discourage, but one needs to deliberately assess all the ramifications before inviting the upheaval that comes from following your dream when your dream is to become a working professional actor

Los Angeles casting directors, taking their marching orders from producers and directors, are in search of not only the best actor for the role but for the actor with "buzz." Who is a hot commodity? Who is an influencer? Who comes to the project with a substantial fan base? Who is a YouTube star? Who is on *Game of Thrones?*

It's very tough to get a strong agent in Los Angeles. Film credits from smaller markets for films that have not gotten distribution or buzz at a film festival mean nothing in Los Angeles. When a Los Angeles agent tells you you don't have enough credits, they mean primetime network, cable, and streaming episodic, and films they've heard of.

If you've just graduated from either high school or college, it's okay if your résumé has no decent credits. However, that window closes around 25 years old. After that, it's a problem. Not to discourage anyone from pursuing this route, but I gotta be honest.

There is plenty of theater in Los Angeles, but the prestige for doing plays just isn't the same as in New York. I don't know why this is the case. I supported Los Angeles theater when I lived there and found so many great actors that way. The level of acting in Los Angeles theater is the same as in New York City. Don't let anyone tell you otherwise.

That being said, many actors got their big break doing small to medium theater in Los Angeles: Chris Pine; Simone Missick (Misty Knight in Marvel's *Luke Cage, The Defenders,* and *Iron Fist;* and now starring in a new show on CBS, *All Rise);* and Diarra Kilpatrick *(American Koko, The Last OG* and the Jordan Peele *Twilight Zone).* There are undoubtedly many more, but I had the good fortune to see these three in particular on those stages and they were all spectacular.

I don't think having a decent car is a prerequisite to living in Los Angeles. I've gone long stints in Los Angeles without a vehicle, one of the periods was over four years. I saved a ton of money by taking public transportation (buses, light rail and subways), walking, biking, using a rideshare service, and catching rides with friends. My stress level went way down because 1) I was never stuck in traffic, 2) I had lots of time to think and catch up on online work, 3) I didn't go anywhere unless it was absolutely necessary, which is a blessing really and not an inconvenience, 4) I arrived early and calm to my destinations because I made a habit of always allowing more time than I think I needed to get there, and 5) I never had to worry about parking. Parking has become a nightmare in Los Angeles in the last five years.

Traveling down the coast as far south as San Diego is easy on Amtrak and the various commuter trains that depart from Union Square downtown. If I absolutely needed a car for a project, I just found the cheapest daily rental rate I could find (Enterprise) and rented a car. My monthly expenses for transportation went from $500+ down to an average of $156 by getting rid of my car. For an actor, that's a lot of money that could otherwise go toward classes, headshots, creating your own content, etc. Los Angeles is a very diverse city with very bright people living in it. It has a lot to offer in regards to culture and recreation, and the weather is ideal.

What Los Angeles is *not* is the Hollywood fantasy of the popular imagination. Los Angeles is a city just like any other, which has people from all walks of life and countries of origin. In fact, only two to five percent of workers in Los Angeles are in entertainment. "Hollywood" is a neighborhood in Los Angeles (and the place where I was born) and it is not glamorous. It's gritty just like any other part of a well trodden

American city. My dad was a refugee and my mom was an immigrant. They were neither rich nor in "the industry." Their story more accurately reflects the reality of Los Angeles and Hollywood than the rags-to-riches stories you've heard.

That being said, there are a lot of great neighborhoods in Los Angeles and you can choose the area to suit your nature. If you enjoy living in an urban environment, then Silver Lake or Echo Park will appeal to your sensibilities (artsy, hip, diverse), and if you prefer a more laid back atmosphere, then Santa Monica, with its wide streets and more casual style, will seem like paradise. You can bike everywhere and the "Blue Bus" system is efficient and very user-friendly.

The cheaper apartments and houses are located in the San Fernando Valley ("The Valley," to locals), much of which is, technically, part of the City of Los Angeles but is separated from downtown, Central LA, and Hollywood by hills and mountains. The temperature is hotter there in the summer and it is not as convenient as living on the Westside (Santa Monica, Marina del Rey, Brentwood, etc.), but it is fine as long as you live close to the hills. There are a lot of studios in the Valley (Warner Brothers, NBCUniversal and Disney are among the bigger ones), so cities like Burbank, Encino, Sherman Oaks, and Altadena are conveniently located to work while also being quiet places to live. I grew up in Burbank; it was a sleepy town then and still is.

As with any city, you can choose to rent an apartment, condo, or house (or buy one if you have a lot of money). You should live someplace that feels like home. Do not share a place with someone you hardly know, and don't stay on someone's couch. Have your own place so you can lead a normal life.

The homeless population in Southern (and Northern for that matter) California has grown exponentially in the last ten years. It's not uncommon to see tent cities pop up in every neighborhood and folks sleeping just outside of expensive restaurants and shops. It's also not uncommon for artists and low-wage workers in the industry to sleep in their cars. If you are uncomfortable with any part of this, you will have a tough time.

New York City also has a homeless population, and is, of course, incredibly expensive in every way ($17 cocktails?!). If you need a lot of space and don't like crowds, New York City is not the place for you. If you can't handle public transportation, don't move here. There is an energy there, however, that is electric and frankly missing in Los Angeles. It's bustling and always teeming with life. As an artist/actor/writer, there is no better place to study humanity, which really should be an artist's lifelong pursuit.

New York City is a great place to be discovered doing stand-up, improv or sketch. And if you are a "triple threat" performer who dreams of being in a Broadway show, you *must* make this place your home—by any means necessary. Most of the actors working in film and episodic TV today came from being on a stage in New York City. Viola Davis, Kate McKinnon, Corey Hawkins, Carrie Coons, Tracey Letts, Rachel Bloom, Corey Stoll, Adam Driver, Marin Ireland, Lupita Nyong'o, Amy Schumer (she even has a theater degree), Denzel Washington (yes, really) and a host of others.

I may be wrong, but my impression is that actors are taken more seriously if they work in New York City. And because the theater, film and television communities are so intertwined in this city, it's very common for actors to go back and forth between live performance and on-camera work, which makes for a very well-rounded career. What's more, the New York City casting directors, agents, and producers go see *everything*. They talk about great performances they've seen with each other, and so if you are great, you will be found.

96

The ideal choices to live are anywhere that is on a New York City subway line or the PATH (Port Authority Trans-Hudson) train, so Hoboken, Jersey City, The Bronx, Queens, and Brooklyn. Although the trains and subways can be extremely crowded and dirty, and they break down probably more than folks would like, it's still an ideal way to get around quickly and not be stuck in traffic, because believe me, you do *not* want to drive in New York City and its environs. Public transportation is so much easier. The money you would put toward a car and all its expenses can go toward your craft (or a better living space).

Atlanta is now in the top three cities for episodic and film production in the world. It's right up there with Los Angeles and New York City. Big network episodic—like *McGyver, The Resident,* and *Dynasty*—shoots here. Netflix, BET, OWN shoots here. All the Marvel movies shoot here. Other types of big studio features were shot here, such as *Little, Love Simon* and *Baby Driver.* The fact is that more big movies are shot here than in Los Angeles.

I came here in 2016 to work on a film and just stayed. It's affordable, walkable, clean and there's a sense of city pride here that's frankly missing in Los Angeles. Oh, and folks complain about the traffic here, but it's *nothing* compared to Los Angeles or New York City. It's like it's so nice here that they need something to complain about.

Despite what you might have heard about the South regarding prejudice and intolerance, Atlanta proper is this bubble of liberalism and inclusivity like no other American city out there. It's a great place for an artist to live no matter what your gender, age, or ethnicity.

Atlanta has great theater, music, the Atlanta Symphony, and outdoor art festivals practically every weekend. The Atlanta Beltline is heaven on earth: a bike- and walkway through the city that is clean and full of art. Along its path, it literally has sculptures, paintings, graphic art, tributes, and whimsical objets d'art. I've honestly never experienced a city with so much art—I use the hashtag "#artiseverywhere" on everything I post about the city. It also has a shockingly good food scene.

Everything is so much easier to go to (the grocery store, a concert, the doctor, urgent care, restaurants, networking events, political rallies, etc.) that it makes one's everyday life so much more pleasant than it would be in either Los Angeles or New York City.

It's not true that actors in Los Angeles of New York City are better than in other cities and actors in Atlanta are amateurs; it couldn't be further from the truth. I've cast and done workshops all over this country, and I've found that the percentage of good and great actors is the same anywhere—about 5% of the total of actors I bring in for a project. Yeah, just 5% I feel are "Wow! I want to cast this actor today!" Not a great percentage but true.

There are basically three tiers. The middle tier is the largest percentage. These are actors that are "okay" or "fine" or "well, with a little rehearsal they could be good." Well, in film and episodic, there is usually no time spent on rehearsing, so this category is not great to be in. The bottom tier actors are just not strong enough to consider under any circumstances. They are either auditioning when they are not ready or just plain too self-conscious to be an actor. But the actors in this group will never hear the words from a casting director, "you're just not good, you should give up acting." We will politely say, "thank you so much," after one take and send them on their way.

Your goal should be to get in that top tier, that 5%.

It's as tough to book acting jobs in Atlanta as in Los Angeles or New York City because of the high standards of these big projects, but Atlanta actors have more opportunities to audition than in either of those cities.

Most auditions in Atlanta are self-tapes, which is why my tips on self-taping are crucial to having a shot at a paying acting gig in film or episodic.

Atlanta has a strong comedy scene, which includes sketch, improv, and stand-up, with a whole host of groups and venues to choose from. The theater in Atlanta is very strong and the audiences for theater are some of the best and most diverse I've ever experienced. There's a theater for any taste—contemporary, experimental, cutting-edge, provocative, classical (Shakespeare), traditional (crowd pleasers such as musicals and American classics)—and I find it extremely stimulating. Frankly, I can't live in a city that doesn't have good theater, so I'm grateful for this one.

Because there are so many actor/artists here now, everyone is working on something, whether it's a short film a friend wrote or a one-woman show that was birthed in a writing class for actors. And because it's cheaper to live here, an actor doesn't have to have three jobs to keep solvent, allowing more time and money toward creation.

Atlantans divide the metro region into two areas: "ITP" ("inside the perimeter," the "perimeter" being I-285), meaning you live within the Atlanta city limits; and "OTP," ("outside the perimeter"), meaning you live in the suburbs. There are neighborhoods for every taste and budget, just like in Los Angeles. Housing prices are, at present, generally about a third of the cost of Los Angeles or New York City.

Your First Six Months in a New City

I know that moving to Los Angeles, New York or Atlanta can seem like a gargantuan task, especially to young actors leaving their hometown for the first time or graduating from college with student loans to pay off.

I am often asked the question, "What do I do once I get to my new home?"

The thing you must *never* do is become complacent. Your first months pursuing acting as a professional are critical to your success and you must not get bogged down by anything other than bettering yourself as an actor.

In the book *Mastery: The Keys to Success and Long-Term Fulfillment*, George Leonard discusses how we *feel* about our chosen profession and how to be successful. He posits that one needs to practice something for at least *five years* in order to master it. Most will give up if they are not making a living at something after five years. This is a shame in the world of acting. Being a successful actor requires practice and patience, just as it is with athletes, musicians, painters, filmmakers, writers, etc.

"The master of any game is the master of practice," states Leonard. Although acting is not a game but an art form, the same rules apply. You practice your game or your art not for any reward but because you love it, and you must practice every day. Do professional athletes work out just when they feel like it? Of course not. Do professional writers just write occasionally, like maybe once a week? No.

The old adage is that "it's not whether you win or lose, it's how you play the game." That also applies to acting. Mastery means always staying on the path, with consistency and discipline. That is *the only way* you will improve. You must love acting so much that you will stick with it no matter what—during the times when you're getting paid to act and during the (possibly) months and years when you're doing it for free. Maybe you're even *paying* to get the chance to act, what with the high cost of classes and the gas it takes to drive to those non-paying jobs.

Masters do not get impatient with the notion of "making it." They just practice what they love, day in and day out, whether they're "feeling it" or not. I contend that you will more likely make it when you completely give up the notion of making it. Besides, what is making it? Your first job on a network episodic show? Your first pilot? Your first series? Your first hit series? Your first feature film role? Or do you need to see your name "above the title" in order to feel that you really made it? The constant pursuit of being successful never ends and it will never be enough if your goal is simply to "make it." Proving to your family, once and for all, that you're worthy despite the fact you chose acting over any other profession in the world is a futile goal. Actors are worthy. You are brave and we admire you for that.

Auditioning is *not* what I mean when I refer to "practice;" an audition is more like a final exam—if you "pass," then you will get a callback. If you practice every day and prepare with all your heart and soul, then you are more likely to get a callback and book a job. You absolutely can't book a job without putting in your time with the boring stuff, much like a musician needs to practice scales. Practicing the boring stuff gets tedious, yes, but if your only opportunity to act is prepping and doing an audition, then your head is not in the right place.

So how can actors practice every day? If he or she is not in rehearsals for a play, performing in a production, booked on an episodic TV show or cast in a film, what is an actor to do?

Take on-camera acting classes. Most actors coming to Los Angeles or New York or Atlanta right out of school have had great theatre training but minimal on-camera experience. You need to feel comfortable in front of the camera before you can feel comfortable in auditions or making self-tapes. In most good on-camera classes you will be taped and the instructor will review the video with you. It's invaluable for you to watch yourself on tape, see what you're doing, and have the chance to improve.

Buy your equipment, tape yourself, and watch your work on a regular basis. If you can't afford an on-camera class right away, you can *create* your own on-camera class. With the price of technology these days, you can find a video camera in any price range or you can use your phone. There's no excuse. Tape yourself doing scenes from plays, or find yourself a new monologue to work on and tape that. Vlog instead of keeping a journal. Write material for yourself. Create a support group of like-minded actors, tape each other, and analyze the work.

Tape and watch yourself every day.

Sign-up for an improv class. As I expressed several times already in this book, the need for comic actors has never been greater and the skill of improvisation has never been more valuable. In Los Angeles and New York City, the best classes are with Upright Citizens Brigade. Introductory classes at UCB—where Amy Poehler cut her comedy teeth—for instance, are about $225 per month with a public performance at the conclusion of each eight-week session. You can't beat the price and the experience! In Los Angeles, there is also The Groundlings, which has probably birthed more SNL stars than any other establishment. A slew of actor/writers who I saw do great work at The Groundlings back in the late '90s are now incredibly successful and had no more experience or contacts in the Industry than you when they arrived in the city: Jim Rash and Nat Faxon (Oscar winners for *The Descendents),* Ben Falcone *(Nobodies, Tammy),* Jennifer Coolidge *(Two Broke Girls).* So many others.

In Atlanta, there are several great improv groups to choose from. Dad's Garage and The Village Theater are bursting with activity. Not a day goes by when either a class or a performance is happening, sometimes several in one day. The Village Theatre has two stages. The average cost a month for classes at either place is $125 (yeah, like I said, Atlanta is more affordable). Before you sign up for the classes, you might want to check out their live shows at any of the venues.

Being new to town, you'll not only learn improv but you'll meet other people with similar goals and creativity and perhaps form friendships for years to come. And who knows, you might be doing your scene with a future comedy writer who could hire you!

Watch episodic shows and films. I'm floored by the percentage of actors I meet who say they don't watch episodic, they don't like it, and they don't know the names of any of the big actors currently working. Since most of the jobs you'll be getting are for episodic, it's best to get over your prejudices now and start watching. With the advent of online viewing of shows, there are really no excuses. Watch old episodes of all formats of episodic shows and analyze them. And don't fast forward through the commercials!

Watch movies in a movie theatre at least twice a month. Movies were made to be seen on the big screen. During my stint teaching at the University of Colorado, Boulder, I made it mandatory that all my students see a first-run film in a movie theatre. I was taken aback that most in the class moaned and groaned about this assignment. I cannot relate to this at all, as my favorite times are sitting in a movie theatre (or live theatre), in the dark, getting lost in the world of the film or play, drawn in by great acting. Is this just a sign of a new generation gap?

Support film and please see a movie in a theatre.

The more you watch, the better you'll understand good acting and the more you'll be aware of current trends in the casting of film and episodic.

Go see theatre and act in plays. Find out what are the best companies in your area. Look up audition notices through *Backstage*, either online or in the weekly hardcopy. Actively participate in the theatre community; yes, even if you strictly want to do film and television. Los Angeles has a great deal of theatre and some of it is very good. Contrary to popular belief, it's not all "showcase theatre." New York City is of course the centerpiece for theater, but Atlanta is also a vibrant hub. Theatre is the best way to keep yourself stimulated between paid acting jobs. Go join one of these, or at the very least, go see their productions. Better yet, form a company with your colleagues from your hometown. Being an actor in either of these cities is not all about "being seen." It's about being a part of a very creative and vibrant artistic community. It's not all about you.

Get a good haircut and buy some new clothes. Feel good about the way you look and wear clothes that are cool, stylish and feel good on your skin. Don't try to be someone you are not, but be the best version of who you are. Yes, this advice is superficial, but it matters.

Get good headshots. The headshots you had in another city will not be good enough for the Los Angeles, New York, or Atlanta markets. I've been to so many different markets and I know what I'm talking about. Don't embarrass yourself by submitting a photo that's not taken by a photographer who specializes in headshot photography. There is an art to headshot photography. These are not portraits. They should not feel posed. Spend the money and do it right away. Don't show your suboptimal headshot to anyone, let alone a casting director at a workshop or an agent you meet through a friend of a friend. You must always show yourself to be classy, smart, and marketable, and your headshot speaks volumes about what kind of actor you are.

Headshots should be in color. Your pose should be relaxed and either a bit flirtatious or deep-in-thought. They should not be too glamorous ("I'm a sexpot") or too severe ("I'm a tough guy cop or criminal"). A natural sexiness always wins out and they eyes are key. It's all about what's going on in your eyes and what you are thinking—because that's what good on-camera acting is all about, as I keep repeating.. If your eyes are dead, if there's nothing going on in them in the photo, we won't be drawn to your headshot.

Before you make your appointment to have headshots taken, make sure you know your branding—what you want your headshot to reflect of you as a person. I would suggest going back to chapter 2 and listing your own dark and light qualities as described. If you don't know who you are, then you won't take a good headshot. Make your list of at least 10–15 emotional qualities and try to reveal at least five of them in a single shot, just as you would in an audition. If your headshots are boring, lifeless, or trying too hard, we won't be attracted to them, just as we won't be attracted to you in your audition or in your self-tapes. Let's look at some examples (headshots by amazingheadshots.com).

(NOTE: Sample headshots are in black and white, yours should be in color.)

BAD

Trying too hard to be a serious actor. Not revealing his true self. Eyes are dead.

GOOD

Eyes are the focus and they're alive, open, naturally sexy; they draw us in.

BAD

Actress is not at all the tough chick she appears to be in this headshot.

GOOD

Her eyes are vulnerable here. Wise and really looking at you. Lovely.

Make sure you choose a headshot photographer who makes you feel comfortable! If you're tense or self-conscious, that will show in your eyes and you will have wasted your money. The lens sees all, and if you're not in the right zone, your photos will reflect this.

You absolutely don't need an "I can be funny" headshot and an "I can be a serious actor" headshot. You really just need one, maybe two really good shots, despite what advice you get from agents or photographers. The one you finally pick to truly represent who you are just needs to be superb. If you're not excited by your headshot, we won't be either. If it doesn't elicit a positive emotional reaction of some kind from us, it won't stand out. Need I remind you? It has to stand out among many hundreds of thumbnail photos.

Make sure your acting résumé is properly formatted. I can guarantee you, the acting résumé you have right now is probably not in the right format. About 95% of the résumés I receive from actors who are just starting to make the rounds as a professional, especially those in smaller markets, are incorrect, and it accentuates the fact that they are an amateur.

Make sure that your acting résumé is current, well-formatted, has no typos (you'd be surprised), and contains either your agent's or manager's contact information or, if you don't have an agent yet, your name, phone number and email address. Forget the elaborate fonts and "objectives." Keep it simple but thorough, accurate and legible.

I've included a basic sample résumé here for you to follow:

ACTOR NAME
SAG-AFTRA (if applicable, otherwise put nothing)
(no need to put small headshot on the resume)
Contact Info or Agency Info

Hair Color: Eye Color: Height:
DOB only if you are under 18

TV

Name of TV Show	Billing	Director

FILM

Name of Film	Billing	Director

NEW MEDIA

Name of Project	Billing	Director

THEATER

Name of Play	Role	Theater Name

COMMERCIALS
Conflicts on Request

TRAINING
List a degree in theater, if you have one, and which college
List a long-term training program next, if applicable
List a month-to-month class next
Don't list one day workshops

SPECIAL SKILLS
List everything you can do. We do look at these!

DON'T FORGET CONTACT INFO!!!!

If you're confused what your billing is on any particular role, it's clearly stated on the contract you received for that job. If it's for an episodic show, for instance, the billing could be *guest star, co-star, recurring,* or *series regular.* For a film, it could be *lead* or *supporting.* For new media, you could also put *lead* or *supporting.*

For theatre jobs, state the name of the role you played, not whether it was supporting or lead. If you played the lead in Harvey, put "Elwood P. Dowd" in the billing column, not "lead."

Under no circumstance should you ever lie or pad your résumé. If you lie on your résumé, you will get caught and it's not worth the risk and discomfort. An actor came in for me once and had on his résumé that he played Andrei in *Three Sisters* at South Coast Repertory in Costa Mesa, California. He listed it as if he had played the leading role on the main stage of that prestigious regional theatre. Because I see a lot of theatre and, in fact, had worked at that theatre in my early years right out of UCLA, I knew he hadn't played Andrei at South Coast Repertory on the main stage. He wasn't experienced or old enough to have played that role. After I questioned him about it, he finally admitted that he did a *scene* from *Three Sisters* in SCR's Adult Conservatory. To make matters worse he got very defensive. This stuff infuriates me. I know how difficult it is to get cast in a lead at a regional theatre. It's disrespectful to your fellow actors and makes you look like a lying fool to misrepresent yourself on our résumé.

You can't list scenes from acting classes as real credits. You can't list extra work, even in smaller markets, even if you were a "featured extra." The credits you can list are those for which you auditioned and the role must have lines. If your lines were cut in the final edit, that's okay, you can still keep that credit, you'll just have to explain what happened if and when you're questioned about it.

If you are under eighteen, provide your date of birth. If you are over eighteen, don't state your age. Also, don't state your weight.

Above all, don't forget to include your email and cell phone number. We need to be able to reach you easily and quickly.

If you're sending your headshot and résumé electronically, please name the file(s) you send with your name, last name first. I can't tell you how many headshots I get via email that are labeled "headshot.jpg" or "IMG_1878.jpg." I get a lot of these—most are requested—and when I download them and they're separated from the email they came attached to, I need to know who's material it is. Duh.

Solidify Your Actors Access Page. Casting Directors interface most with your Actors Access page and your IMDB. We really don't have time to also visit your website and highly likely won't go past the home page. But your Actors Access page is the source with which we choose if you get an audition or not.

Some of my pet peeves about this page are the following:

1) If you have too many "looks"—i.e., if there are too many headshots—I'll get confused.

2) Make sure your headshots are current and look like you *now*, at *this* point in time. It's irritating when I give a slot to an actor based on their headshot and the person who self-tapes or auditions in person doesn't resemble the headshot. It's a wasted slot, and every slot is precious.

3) Glamorous headshots can be deceiving. Too much retouching is just a waste of our time. If you appear too far afield from your image, you will get on our bad side. I also don't think you need more than two headshots. One "commercial" and one "theatrical" is pretty much it. When you or your agent submits you, they will click on the headshot that's most appropriate for the role. When we open up the submission, we see everything, all the headshots. Make it easy on us. When we give you a slot, we want to see what's accurately represented.

4)   Your **media** needs to be current, short-and-sweet and to-the-point. My preference is to watch a **one-minute** demo reel because, frankly, we won't watch past a minute of anything; and—as with self-taped auditions—if you don't grab us in the first 10 seconds, we won't continue watching to the end anyway. If you do choose to have more than one source of media, just make sure your demo reel is listed first, and that the short clips you also include are clearly labeled—"comedy clip" or "drama clip". As with your headshots, make sure your media is current and represents who you are now. Your demo reel should favor *you* and no other actors. Your face, your close-up should be the first image we see. In fact, the best is a meta shot. We don't need to understand the context, we don't need to see full scenes. You want to provide snippets of your on-camera work so we can assess your acting, your essence and what you look like now. We don't want to see old footage. If the acting is weak, don't use it—yes even it's the only thing you have. This media is often the first impression we get of you. Make it a strong one.

5)   "Slate Shots" with your headshots, where you simply state your name, should be natural and relaxed. Don't be formal, don't try too hard, don't try to be cute or serious, just be authentic.

6)   The "Represented By" section has gotten more complicated in the last five years. Prior to the Southeast market explosion, an actor usually had either a Los Angeles agent or a New York City agent. They might have had a manager as well. In looking at their representation, we knew where they lived, where they were based. If we were looking for a "local hire" only—which is usually the case for co-star roles—we were pretty certain they were actually local to the city we needed them in. Now,

when I go to someone's page, I undoubtedly will see several reps, in all three regions—a CA rep, a NY rep and a GA rep. And, as an added bonus, they might have a manager in Florida. So which rep should I contact to set up the audition? Remember, I'm having to cover a lot of ground in a limited time, so I want this process to be easy, a no-brainer. It is seldom that anymore. And an even bigger question looms, however: "where do they live?" "Local hire" means the actor *lives* within 500 miles of the city in which the shoot takes place. If an actor is hired under these conditions, production will not pay for travel, accommodations, a per diem, or ground transportation. Production will just expect you to show up, on time, to your wardrobe fitting and when you are scheduled to be on set. There is no wiggle room whatsoever if you can't guarantee 100% you can show up at the drop of a hat and on your dime. Production has *no* patience for something going awry that is the actor's fault. And who also gets blamed for this? The casting director. We hate this. And we will remember you.

The ideal circumstances for being hired as a local if you're not really a local include the following:

a. You have a residence with a real address (not a hotel) in that city

b. You have great transportation

c. You don't expect reimbursement for meals, mileage or gas

d. You can be there at the drop of hat, no matter what production asks of you

e. You fully disclose to the casting director that you don't live in the city but that you can be considered local hire with the aforementioned stipulations.

Any other scenario is extremely risky, not only for the short-term headaches that will inevitably arise, but for the long term relationships you have with the casting director and your representation. If *anything* goes wrong (like the shoot dates change and they need you there tomorrow morning at 6am and there's bad weather in your path), production will be incensed with us because, like us, they are over-stressed, overworked, and on a fast-moving train that feels like it could go off the rails at any moment. The last thing they want to worry about is an actor who is not the star.

This doesn't mean you can't get hired to work in Atlanta if you live in Los Angeles. It happens all the time, especially for guest star roles in episodic or supporting roles in films—you simply get hired as a Los Angeles-based actor. Production takes care of your travel arrangements and expenses, flies you first class (a SAG-AFTRA rule), provides first-class hotel accommodations, gives you a per diem, takes care of ground transportation in both cities, and basically provides support such that all you have to do is know your lines and show up. There is no stress in this scenario. All the responsibilities and costs are borne by others.

The financial cost to you can be substantial if you insist on submitting yourself as a local hire when you're not, and the competition is stiffening: there is currently a big push in Atlanta to foster the great actors that actually live here, of which there are many. The percentage is as high as in Los Angeles or New York City as I mentioned previously. Casting directors who have committed to living and working in their community will always go for the actual local actors first. It's easier on everyone and really makes more sense.

There are, of course, exceptions to these rules, and with the rise of self-taping, casting has gotten more global. Just be smart, responsible, and transparent. Don't expect anyone to cover for you if something goes wrong.

10) The format of your résumé in Actors Access should be similar to that of the print version—television should go first, then film, then theater, etc. Your training section should be concise, as described above.

11) Don't add a section in which you tell us more about you, like "I'm a dynamic performer who is dedicated to the craft." This is trying too hard. Let your work stand on its own.

12) List as many skills as you can in which you are proficient. Make this comprehensive but not padded.

Register your car and obtain a driver's license in the city in which you live. You are there to stay.

Contact everyone you know who knows someone who knows someone who lives in the city you've chosen. Tell them you have moved and would like their advice on everything from getting an agent to the best bar in town. There is so much help out there for you; all you need do is ask. That's how I got my first casting job. Once I decided what I wanted to do and "put it out there in the universe", I contacted my good friend Julie Haber who happened to go to college with Jeff Greenberg, one of the very top casting directors in Los Angeles. His big credit prior to *Frasier* was *Cheers,* my favorite sitcom ever. From that contact Jeff hired me and the rest is history. That all happened in a matter of months, once I asked for help.

Put yourself out there. What you're doing is important, valuable, and requires all your effort. But don't be annoying. Don't pester anyone. Keep it cool and real, just like your acting should be.

Don't rush to get an agent or audition. I know you want to "hit the ground running" and get an agent and start auditioning as soon as you arrive in your new city. But "hitting the ground running" sounds painful and ill-advised. Believe me when I urge you to *settle in* with your day-to-day life before reaching out to any agencies or casting directors. These initial communications and meetings will be fraught with anxiety and uncertainty. It's just the nature of the beast. You want this so badly, you're willing to do and say anything, to put on any persona that will get you signed or be given the opportunity to "show your stuff." You absolutely can't be meeting anyone in the industry with that kind of affect, that nervous energy. First impressions do matter. If you are still reeling from the big move, don't combine that uneasiness with the uneasiness of meeting some who could change your life.

Find your new coffee place, dry cleaner and market. Exercise. Join a gym. Take your time to unpack and set up your living space just as you desire, in order to feel comfortable. Check out a comedy club. Reach out to folks you might already know in the area. Select a new doctor. Find your new hair stylist. You'll highly likely be looking for a day job—and that's stressful enough as it is! The goal of this "settling in" period is to find your new center so that you will be able to reveal your true relaxed self when you do have the opportunity to meet someone who will help you reach your goals.

Explore the city! Los Angeles, Atlanta, and New York are cities with so much to offer that isn't related to the business. They are overflowing with museums, historical architecture and monuments, universities, and parks. Take a walking tour of historical downtown Los Angeles. Go to Union Station and catch a subway (yes, there is a subway in Los Angeles!) or train going anywhere—north, south, east or west. Walk the Belt line in Atlanta and take in the art and music festivals in the city's varied neighborhoods—they are numerous. In New York, walk from Battery Park all the way up to Central Park. It's amazing how many worlds you will walk through in just a few hours.

Enjoy. You have taken the plunge and are pursuing the profession that you desire. Don't fret over the little things and don't complain about the traffic or the subway system. In fact, I will go out on a limb now by stating that if you suffer from impatience and "sweat the small stuff," you probably shouldn't pursue acting professionally.

Don't audition for *everything*. I think it's good to do student films made at USC, NYU or SCAD. It's good to do a short film that has a great script. What's not good is to do anything and everything out there that comes your way, thinking you can build up your résumé with just random credits. Working on an amateur project with a mediocre script and a first-time director will get you nowhere and nothing—not even good experience. Most amateur projects are not run well or cast well, and, worse, you might pick up bad habits without realizing it. As I keep saying, the only credits that truly mean anything are high-end episodic and feature films under the SAG-AFTRA banner that get distribution. Good credits are those from network and cable episodic, the major streaming services and films that actually play in the local movie theater. Honestly, most indie projects are at best a waste of time and money and at worst demoralizing. Your focus should always be on getting cast in an episodic show you've heard of, a quality pilot that is already picked up by a network, and a film with a superior script. If you can't get auditions for these kinds of projects right off the bat, don't fret, be patient—if you're talented, have a great attitude, and reveal yourself to everyone you meet, the auditions will

116

come. Don't spin your wheels doing crap. Instead, go create your own content.

7 SOCIAL MEDIA AND BEING AN INFLUENCER

I sometimes wish we could go back to the day when all an actor had to do was act, but that will never happen.

"Do you really care about how many followers I have?" I get asked this question a lot. There is not a simple answer.

If I've seen you perform and love what you did, I don't care how many followers you have. Undoubtedly, however, the mid-level producer or the network or platform head might. As you are perhaps well aware, there's an overabundance of content now. The producer, in order to capture more eyeballs, will be happy if you have a built-in audience already in place. Sure, they might insist on hiring that YouTube star over you, but like everything else, you have no control over this so there's no use stressing over it.

What you *do* have control over is your outlook on this new monster known as online content and social media. Instead of seeing it as a chore —"why do I have to be on social media? I'm a private person. Isn't it a waste of time, my time?"—because frankly, if you have this opinion, you will have a hard time. It is true, you must have an online presence now. Before you give up on the acting profession in frustration, however, I suggest you turn it around and start thinking of yourself as an *influencer*. An influencer is one who offers others a new perspective on the world. To "influence" means to have an effect on the character, development, or behavior of someone or something. Isn't that what artists *do?* Why should that, then, be a chore?

Actors, performers, musicians, storytellers want to change the world for good—or at least they should, otherwise, why be an artist? It's an axiom in the industry that you can't be pursuing an acting career just for the fame and fortune. It's a damn hard road and not to be taken lightly.

Being an actor is a privilege. It allows you a platform to change the world. Why not take full advantage of that?

Let me explain how to use your platform, which is your branding, in the most positive way.

Your branding should reveal the true you (just like with good acting) and not a fake version of yourself. Your social media posts should not scream "Look at me! Look at me! Aren't I great?"

The best strategy for social media posts is one of balance and integrity. Balance your posts about what you are doing in the industry with posts about how you see the world, your point of view on life. If you have no life outside of the industry, then your acting will suffer.

A good balance is:

1) Three posts where you ask for something or promote a service or product

2) Three posts where you share what you are working on currently

3) Four posts where you reveal an aspect of your real life, your true story.

The latter is the most important because stories are all we've got. "Selling yourself" is one thing, but *sharing yourself* is what will connect you best with others.

Humans are starved for good stories. Despite what is reflected in a lot of media content this days, we are interested in real stories—not those

121

that are over-sensationalized or titillating. We watch movies to be moved, to feel something, to not feel so alone. Let Hollywood make the big, sensational action films. In your own work, you can't compete with that. You simply don't have the budget.

Tell your *own* real story. A great story doesn't need to be sensationalized for it to be interesting. Our real stories help others not feel so alone, they foster empathy and compassion. With all the negative stereotype images and talk, we all need something different. *You*, who are pursuing the acting profession, have the platform and capacity to help this along.

Telling your own story also helps the monotony of being cast in co-star roles, none of which allows you the platform to show what you can really do. I call these "utilitarian roles"—the cop, the nurse, the lawyer, the waiter. There are more of these roles than any other type for an actor who's not a star already. In fact, it's the bread-and-butter of making money as an actor. Getting three lines on *The Resident* is harder than you might imagine. It's thrilling to get booked on an episodic TV show or in a film no matter the size of the role, but, in the end, are you pursuing acting to play the utilitarian roles? I would think not.

Create Your Own Content

Let me use my own story as an example. I was born in Hollywood—a Los Angeles native—and worked for years in the entertainment industry. The stereotype of someone with such a history is the fake, privileged woman, a child of wealthy parents who were, themselves, probably in the industry. Her career came easily from all her connections, she drives a

BMW (or, nowadays, a Prius), etc. This description could not be further from the truth.

My father was a refugee who suffered from severe PTSD before it was called that. He died when I was 12. My mom was an immigrant who worked minimum-wage jobs until she died in her 70s. Both were uneducated and, in fact, I'm the first person in my family to graduate from college, going back through all generations on both sides. Neither parent was in the industry. I currently drive a 2011 Ford Focus. I do not shop at Whole Foods and I've never had botox. I don't own any property. I went years with no health insurance. I have no retirement savings. I've never had grandparents or an extended family. *Everything* that I've accomplished has been from sheer will power, determination, resilience and just a plain ol' blind faith in the power of film, theater, music, books —stories. I was not blessed with a strong family unit but thank God for the angels He has provided me throughout my life.

For *years* I hid my story out of shame and insecurity. In doing so, I was leading an inauthentic life. During the years that I was "succeeding" in the upper echelons of casting, I felt out of place, unworthy of living in so rarefied a world. This subconsciously kept me back from fully expressing myself. I supported other people's stories but never my own.

My story is unique, just as yours is. I have written and spoken extensively about my life and family history, which includes the Holocaust, and in doing so, I feel I have enriched other people's lives as well as my own. You could say my story *humanizes* Hollywood and the industry. Perpetuating the negative stereotypes of any group, place, religion, or gender diminishes us all. My DIY projects have all been, at their core, about deconstructing these negative stereotypes. My social media posts reflect my unique view of the world I live in, without being militant about it.

I have told my story in different contexts, in different genres—short stories, film scripts, testimonies, motivational speeches, and yes, even stand-up. I resisted having the Holocaust as a subject in my stand-up. Who's going to laugh at a joke about the gas chambers? A kind and knowledgeable stand-up coach at Flappers Comedy Club in Burbank emphatically told me, "the Holocaust *is* the story." He shared that comics are always looking for that subject, that story that makes them unique, helps them stand out from the crowd. Who knew that I had a built-in crowd-grabber all along that I had been afraid to use? Sure enough, when I relented and switched up my routine, my jokes related to the Holocaust and how it impacted me and my family always got laughs.

Tell your story in the mode that feels most comfortable for you.

Creating your own content doesn't have to be an overwhelming endeavor. Some projects will take awhile and cost money but there are many ways that are simple and can be shot and edited in two days.

Lena Dunham wrote, produced, and starred in a low-budget indie (*Tiny Furniture*) that put her on the map. Bo Burnham (*Eighth Grade*), who was the youngest comedian to ever perform on *Comedy Central Presents,* created no-budget videos in his bedroom and posted them on YouTube. The early videos Donald Glover posted while he was in college are downright embarrassing, and yet his undeniable charisma and POV shines through. Mindy Kaling co-wrote and starred in a play (*Matt and Ben*) in 2003 that got the notice of NBC. Tiffany Haddish's early videos captured from the stage of The Laugh Factory in Los Angeles are a wonder to behold. Why it took her so long to get "discovered" is incomprehensible.

Issa Rae, Mike Birbiglia, John Leguizamo, Whoopie Goldberg, and Tyler Perry, for God's sake, all created their own content, which got them discovered and now Tyler Perry owns a studio! None of these performers fit easily into an established "type" when they were starting out. They each created their own niche.

Can you imagine any of these superstars getting discovered had they just taken classes and auditioned?

So many actors I meet lament, "but I don't know how to write!" You know how to write. We all do. We've had to write our entire lives! We write school assignments, emails, posts, applications for college and documents for work. You can write. Just start small. Write a scene between you and your alter ego. I call this "The Play About the Saboteur." It's simply a scene in which you grapple with your alter ego, your imaginary "evil twin." You can even write a scene in which you wrestle with your negative chatter on the subject of having to write a scene in which you wrestle with your negative chatter!

TRUE YOU

I'm going to do this. I'm going to
write a scene in which I'm the lead.

SABOTEUR

What are you kidding? You're an
idiot. Just a stupid actor. You don't
know how to write.

TRUE YOU

Why do you torture me like this? I'm
a good person, a good actor.

SABOTEUR

You are a nobody. You've been chasing
this dream for five years. Look at
all the money you've spent, the time
you've put into it, the relationships
you've squandered. For what? You live
with five guys in a one-bedroom
apartment.

TRUE YOU

So what? I'm having a blast. That
impromptu improv show we created last
night was pee-in -your-pants funny.
Thank God we videotaped it. I'm gonna
post it today.

SABOTEUR

Oh, dear Lord. That won't get you an
audition, it will get you arrested.

TRUE YOU

Look, Saboteur or evil twin or
whatever your damn name is! Cut the
crap. This negative chatter is
bullshit and I just can't take it
anymore.

SABOTEUR

Yeah, the truth hurts, don't it.

TRUE YOU grabs SABOTEUR'S arm in an
unexpected aggressive move and twists it
behind his back.

                    TRUE YOU
        It's about time you learned your
        place in this world, MY world, and
        it's not here out in the open.

TRUE YOU opens the closet door and shoves
SABOTEUR into the closet. He immediately
slams the door shut and locks it. SABOTEUR
pounds on the door.

                  SABOTEUR (O.C.)
        What the hell! Are you crazy?? You
        can't do anything without me. I keep
        you in line!!

TRUE YOU throws away the key out the
window and goes about his day, leaving
SABOTEUR pounding and yelling from inside
the closest.

You get the picture. It's a fun exercise and you will have no trouble
writing this scene. You are well aware of your negative chatter—it's with
you constantly (and that's the problem). You need to write about your
saboteur so you can have a better relationship with that beast. You'll never
get rid of it, but you can tame it by simply giving it a platform from which
to speak out.

Some actors I've given this assignment to have made their saboteur play into a short video in which they play both roles. It's not only a great exercise but undoubtedly will create a very entertaining video to post that everyone can relate to. I mean, who on this earth doesn't have a saboteur? Sure, posting it will perhaps make you feel vulnerable and insecure. But isn't that the point? An actor who doesn't go out on a limb and truly reveal himself is not a strong actor.

The medium or format for your own content can be anything. A one-act play, a solo show, a scene, a short film script, a feature-length screenplay, stand-up, spoken word, rap, playing a musical instrument, singing, singing in the shower… really anything. Don't limit yourself and don't stress over it too much, just find what feels most right to you and *begin*.

In *La La Land,* Mia (Emma Stone) creates her own content as a one woman show due to Sebastian's proddings and she becomes a star because of it. When Sebastian "sells out" by going on the road with a band, Mia reminds him of his own dream of owning a jazz club. "Please will want to go to it because you're passionate about it. And people love what other people are passionate about. "

8 YOU ARE AN ENTREPRENEUR

As I keep stressing, you won't succeed being just an actor for hire. But you are more than a business—you are a start-up. You are an *entrepreneur.* So what does that mean?

The current Merriam-Webster dictionary has a simple answer—"a person who starts a business and is willing to risk loss in order to make money." This definition absolutely applies to actors—as we all know by now, actors have to invest money in a whole lot of expenses before they can even think about getting an agent and auditioning. Some actors *never* make a profit. This fact does not seem to stop the diehards from pursing this business.

If you are one of those diehards, be smart about it. Be a go-getter, embrace the *entrepreneurial spirit,* which is one of great insight, innovation, creativity, risk-taking, and discipline. In the non-acting business world, the traits that support an entrepreneur are:

1) Have **passion** for the business

2) Be **authentic**

3) Get **experience**

4) **Ask** for help

5) Be **social online**

6) Use **live video**

7) **Network** in person

8) **Pitch yourself** to media

9) How badly do you **want** it?

10) Always **learn and improve** your skills

All of these traits absolutely apply to the professional actor.

What also applies to the acting profession, unfortunately, is that a significant proportion of start-up businesses have to close due to lack of funding, bad business decisions, an economic crisis, lack of market demand, or a combination of all of these.

So we can now all agree, you own a business.

Start with the basics. Have the most up-to-date equipment and subscriptions: computer, iPhone, printer, set-up for self-taping (as discussed previously), and editing software that's easy to use like iMovie. Maintain a current ActorsAccess, profile, IMDb page, and a subscription to IMDb Pro. Have a Casting Networks account if your agent requests it. At the very least, have Facebook, Instagram, and Twitter accounts.

Have "**office hours**" for all things related to your art and stick to it. This time is sacrosanct. It could be 10am–2pm each weekday. It could be 11am–1pm. It could even be a half-hour every morning. Just make it something you can stick to and that works well with your day-job hours. Don't go crazy. If you are fortunate enough not to need a day job, don't say you will treat acting like a nine-to-five. That's too many hours. Half of that time will be wasted (just as it is in most nine-to-five jobs in the corporate world).

Make a list of your top five **goals** related to acting. This list could include something as basic as "book a co-star role on a network or streaming episodic" all the way to "performing a comedy special at Carnegie Hall." It could also include "make enough money as an actor to be able to quit my day job" or "do stand up twice a week at a respected venue." This list should, of course, include "write and help produce a short film where I am the lead." Whatever you want, whatever you know you can stick to, just write it down: **Top Five Goals.** Don't make this list in haste. Pray on it, meditate on it, whatever you need to do to dig deep in your soul and figure out truly what you want to attain and why the heck your are doing this in the first place.

Make a list of your top three **priorities**, in order of importance. Making this list is important because most actors in the early phases of their careers will put "acting" at the top of the list. This is extremely shortsighted and narrow in scope. I urge you to look at this in a more holistic way, where the "whole is greater than the sum of its parts." For instance, where does "self-care" go on the list? Or "solvency"? What about "family," "God," "home"?

This list gets very tricky, as you can see, but is worth the effort in the long run, as it provides focus and clarity. Let's call it GPS for not only your career but for your life.

Priority List Labels (just a sample—make up your own)

Home	Work (day job)	Having Purpose
Solvency	Artistic Life	Spiritual pursuits
Self-Care	Acting	Relaxing
Intimate Relationships	Doing Good In The	
Family	World	

Who are you at your core? What do you hold dear? Create a list of your top five **values**—values that run so deep in you that if any one of them were compromised you would suffer. When you are first starting out in the industry, you want to succeed so badly you are willing to do almost anything.

Nip this in the bud now.

If you have been a working actor for some time and feel you have given up a piece of your soul, making this list will be a chance to regroup and, ideally, regain your joy.

Here's a general list to help you begin.

Achievement	Friendships	Physical challenge
Advancement and promotion	Growth	Pleasure
Adventure	Having a family	Power and authority
Affection (love and caring)	Helping other people	Privacy
Arts	Helping society	Public service
Challenging problems	Honesty	Purity
Change and variety	Independence	Quality of what I take part in
Close relationships	Influencing others	Quality relationships
Community	Inner harmony	Recognition (respect from others, status)
Competence	Integrity	Religion
Competition	Intellectual status	Reputation
Cooperation	Involvement	Responsibility and accountability
Country	Job tranquility	Security
Creativity	Knowledge	Self-Respect
Decisiveness	Leadership	Serenity
Democracy	Location	Sophistication
Ecological awareness	Loyalty	Stability
Economic security	Market position	Status
Effectiveness	Meaningful work	Supervising others
Efficiency	Merit	Time freedom
Ethical practice	Money	Truth
Excellence	Nature	Wealth
Excitement	being around people who are open and honest	Wisdom
Fame	Order (tranquility, stability, conformity)	Work under pressure
Fast living	Personal development	Work with others
Financial gain	Freedom	Working alone

Start practicing better **time management**. Make a thorough list of all the activities you do in a given day or week. You must include eating, exercise, doing laundry, cleaning the bathroom—mundane tasks as well as bigger ones like "Monday class" and "time with loved one." Every one of these tasks *take time,* and usually more than you allot. How much time do you spend on social media? How much time do you spend driving places? How much time do you spend preparing meals? Day-to-day existence needs to be chronicled in minute detail because it all takes time and we don't have an unlimited amount in a given day.

Creating this assessment of the tasks you need to schedule helps you look long and hard at exactly how you spend your days. Only by doing this can you then go through the list and remove those tasks, those commitments, those relationships that don't serve you well. Being an entrepreneur artist takes laser focus and taps into all the resources you have. Time is the most valuable commodity. Use it wisely.

Have a "To Do" list.

Write everything down.

Get organized. How much time is wasted just finding things, numbers, email addresses, the notes you took at that last workshop?

Don't overbook your days. You never know when you well get an audition and have to self-tape. The last thing you want to do is have to scramble every time you have a precious audition. Heaven forbid in your mad scramble you also have to cancel all the things you had scheduled because you overbooked yourself.

Say "no" more than you say "yes." If you are a giver, this will be difficult.

Create clear boundaries with others who aren't in your intimate circle.

Overextending and stressing yourself is the worst thing you can do, for your health and your art. Believe me. I did that for years and it made me sick.

Make time to be by yourself, unplugged. Regeneration time is golden.

Find more time for your art and less time for running around doing errands. Make the locations of your errands close to where you live. Don't use errands as a procrastination technique.

Be stingy on the time you spend helping other artists create their art.

Notice what sidetracks you—going out every night socializing, being on a committee, joining a social club, networking events where you don't feel comfortable…. You don't have to go to everything, be everywhere, appear in every friend's project. You have priorities and if you don't respect them, your artistic cocoon will unravel.

I have known many talented actors who have spent *years* wasting their time getting sidetracked. It's pretty sad. Don't let this happen to you.

Find a side job that makes you the most money for the least amount of time. If you work in the restaurant industry, insist on only three shifts a week and don't take on anyone else's when they ask.

Don't get sucked into other people's drama. Keep the drama in only in your art.

What is your biggest time waster? Sometimes just being mindful of our distractions can help eliminate them.

Organize your finances. Since you are a business owner, you should have two bank accounts—one for personal and one for business. All of your income (even your day job salary) should go into the business account and then you will pay yourself a salary by transferring money into your personal account. Keep track of *every single expense* on whatever format you like best—Quickbooks, Excel spreadsheets, etc. Don't wait until the end of the year to input all your receipts! Pick a day each week, as part of your office hours, and input all of your amounts into your accounting software. This practice will not only make your life so much easier during the dreaded tax time, but will also force you to look at your financial health in a consistent, direct, and truthful way. Don't go into denial about how and when you spend your money. Doing so will put your whole house of cards (i.e., your dreams) in jeopardy. Remember, "solvency" should definitely be in your top three priorities.

It's rare when an actor has consistent full-time work. Even series regulars have months off from their series, and a show could get cancelled at any time. It's imperative you save a portion of your earnings while you are working, in anticipation of the inevitable slow times. This is true if you have a consistent day job as well. There is nothing worse than being caught short and having to borrow money from a friend or family member. Believe me, I've been there. It's great that folks want to help, but it's also demoralizing. Note that I am not talking here about accepting money from a friend or family member who wants to support you in your specific endeavors, kind of like a sponsor. In this context, support means you won't have to pay back the money. You have reached out for support *ahead of time* versus having your back to the wall and feeling desperate.

I highly recommend *The Profit Handbook: The Entrepreneur's Guide to Grow Business and Personal Wealth* by Patricia Stallworth. Stallworth is so special and her financial acumen is transforming people's lives in ways they didn't think possible. She *wants* you to succeed and helps you take a good hard look at your financial health with no judgement—only compassion and deep insight.

Grapple with your **self-trust issues.** Those who constantly doubt their own judgement are especially prone to a wide range of psychological problems, such as mood swings, low self-esteem, anxiety, and depression.

9 PILOT SEASON

In my two previous editions of this book, I had a whole section devoted to pilot season. For more than 20 years, pilot season never really changed. With the onslaught of streaming and on-demand, however, the networks have had to adapt, and adapt they have. The new landscape related to episodic is now ever-changing. I have a strong feeling that this updated section on pilot season will probably be outdated in two years. Perhaps it's becoming outdated as you read this.

I questioned whether to even bother including this section. Pilot season used to be great, but, even then, only for a chosen few. Booking a pilot your first season out was like winning the lottery, and it still is. I don't think actors should concentrate on pilot season at all, especially now when studios are going after more well-established and star actors than ever before. If you get an audition for a new episodic pilot, great, but it's not something you should obsess over if you don't.

What you should concentrate on is booking co-star, guest star, and recurring roles for episodic, in order to build strong credits on your résumé and for the top echelon casting directors to get to know you. If you are a known commodity, you will then more likely get the opportunity to audition for a series regular. Being a series regular—meaning that, contractually, you are in every episode produced,—is how an actor can (finally) make substantial money. That should be a goal. Breaking into this rarefied group is tough and truly takes a lot of hard work, but once you've been a series regular, the auditions come easier and for better and better roles. Notice how it seems the same actors keep getting cast in new shows? You want to be in that category.

The good news is episodic—where you build these credits—is now a year-round proposition. There are no breaks. There is no such thing as a "hiatus" when Los Angeles or New York City would shut down between May and July or August. Networks used to air original episodes from fall to spring, at which time reruns kicked in. Networks now have originals year-round and on-demand is the new rerun.

The show order for network shows used to be 13/9—the networks would initially order 13 episodes of any given series, and if the series did well or the show runner was well-liked by the network, they would order the "back nine;" so a full order added up to 22 episodes. A series regular would work on all 22. This is still true for some series *(The Resident, Mom)*.

One of the reasons for this new normal of year-round activity is that networks now need to compete with streaming services, so they are in constant need of original episodes. Series orders have therefore become flexible. With a "pickup"—when a pilot becomes a series—the order could be 22 episodes (the 13/9 formula), but now is more likely to be 13, 10, or 8, along the lines of cable show orders. When an anchor series airs all 22 original episodes, for instance, the networks now need to schedule a 10 episode show to fill the slot that used to be reruns.

Pilot season really was a big deal and some actors organized their lives around it, hoping for that big break. Actors and their families who went out to Los Angeles only for pilot season found a very treacherous and costly road, however. Let's say you were a young female actress who can play between the ages of twelve and fifteen. You went out for pilot season with your family on a particular year and it turns out that, for that pilot season, the shows did not happen to have roles in your age range. You did not know that that was going to be the case until you were already out there and the breakdowns started coming out. It would have been frustrating to say the least. The pressure to book a pilot can be a heavy burden, especially for a young actor; it is even more so if you can't even get the opportunity to book one. For an adult actor who went out for

141

pilot season with no strong connections to Los Angeles casting directors —or worse, no agent or manager—it was honestly a fool's errand.

To give you some context, this is what pilot season used to be (and in some cases still is, but in a very limited fashion).

In December and January, a casting director with a great track record with pilots and series was hired by a studio. The casting office created a breakdown of the script for Breakdown Services. The breakdown provided the following information: names of those producing, writing, and directing the pilot; the network and studio; the type of show (hour drama, multiple-camera sitcom, etc.); when the pilot will shoot and in what city; and, most importantly, complete character descriptions and requirements for all the roles to be cast. To give you a sense of the numbers, a typical hour drama pilot had as many as ten series regulars that needed to be cast.

Casting directors not only had to find actors for all of the series regulars roles for a pilot, but they also had to fill the co-star and guest star roles in that episode. That could add up to twenty actors for a pilot. The casting director traditionally had up to ten weeks to cast all the roles, but that got whittled down to four in later years.

During pilot season, which was traditionally January through March, there was a *lot* of casting going on. It was a crazy, hectic time in which actors in high demand could be going out for two or three pilot auditions in a single day.

The order of the audition process for any given pilot was as follows:

1)   Pre-read with the casting director.

2)   Callbacks for the producer/creator of the show.

3) A second callback for the producer, at which time the producer would make very sure they liked this actor.

4) If the actor makes it past the second callback, then the network/studio starts a *test deal option*. The test deal option starts negotiations between the agent representing the actor and the business affairs department of the network. The two parties negotiate everything from billing to compensation for the pilot and for the series, and, should the pilot go to series, dressing rooms, relocation fees, etc. This negotiation will lead to a contract that usually covers five to seven years. An actor works closely with his or her agent at this point as the agent negotiates with business affairs on the actor's behalf.

The actor signs this contract before going in to test at the studio. This test is in front of the executives at the show's studio. Some examples of studios are Fox 21 Television, Universal Television, and ABC Studios. The executives that are present at the test are the studio president, the VP of development, the VP of casting, the manager of casting, and the manager of development who has been assigned to this particular show at that studio. It's a nerve-wracking audition and I've seen brilliant actors crumble under the pressure. The actor only gets this one chance. Those who do not do a great audition will not be hired. If it is for a comedy role and the actor doesn't get a laugh, they won't get hired.

If the actor does a great audition and if the executives fall in love with this actor, then the actor proceeds to the final audition in this grueling process—the network test, at which the actor will audition for the network's president, VP of development, VP of casting, manager of casting and so on; as well as all the studio executives who were at the previous test.

Most of the time, there are three or four different actors vying for any one role. Some actors get cut at this point, which is when the process gets really heartbreaking. Many, many fine actors through the years and years of pilot seasons were cut at this point. It does not mean they never worked again! They moved on and thrived. However, an actor not "released" at this point survives to the final round.

At the completion of the network test, only one actor gets hired, obviously, for each role in the pilot. The executives of the studio and network see the auditions back to back and choose who they like the best. Sometimes they do not choose anyone and the casting director has to start back at square one for that role. "We have to see more people," is about the *worst* thing a casting director can be told at the end of a network test. This is when we have to go back to our office, tails between our legs, and start from scratch.

If an actor is chosen at this point, he or she becomes "attached" to the show and will shoot the pilot as a series regular, if it gets shot. There have been some cases where a pilot is stalled or, worse was dead on arrival because casting couldn't be completed (e.g., for lack of a strong lead).

Los Angeles was the base for pilot casting, but the networks would hire casting directors from across the country and around the world in order to widen the net. If an actor they found sparked the interest of the Los Angeles casting directors and executives, they would get flown first class to Los Angeles for the studio and network tests. In 2018, I was hired by NBC Universal to put actors on tape in Atlanta. It was a first for that city and very exciting for the whole community. One actor, Brick Jackson, made it all the way to the network test for *Abby's*. He came in second. We were of course all disappointed, but, still, it's no small feat to get even that far in the process.

Once a pilot is cast and shot, the finished product is delivered to the studio and network along with all the other pilots made during that pilot season. Some networks made ten to twenty pilots. All the pilots are assessed and it is at this time that the networks decide which of the pilots will go to series. It is also at this time that the actors who appeared in pilots find out whether they will have the good fortune to work on a series. The final announcements are unveiled at the *upfronts* which take place in New York City in mid-May. This is a huge event when all the advertisers, media buyers, and episodic television critics come to see what the new fall season will look like. Series production on the pilots that are picked up usually begins in July (for hour-longs) and August (for sitcoms).

Most of the pilots that get made are never seen by the general public.

Here is a partial list of pilots I worked on as a casting director that never went forward:

Sick in the Head, Fox (1998)—created by Judd Apatow, starred David Krumholtz and Kevin Corrigan. Amy Poehler, before she did SNL, was a guest star on the pilot. Probably the funniest pilot ever made.

All About Us, CBS—three couples all at various stages of a relationship. Yeah, it was pretty generic. It was tough finding the male leads, as is most often the case. They have to be naturally funny, attractive, and likable.

Say Uncle, CBS—starred Ken Olin as a gay uncle who becomes the guardian to his sister's children after she's tragically killed in a car accident. Teri Hatcher was so great (she did this show before she got *Desperate Housewives* which rejuvenated her career). Michael Angarano and Daveigh Chase were the kids and they were both brilliant.

Misconceptions, The WB—Jane Leeves played a single mother who, thirteen years prior, had gone to a sperm back in order to conceive

145

her child. Now that anonymous donor comes into her life. Taylor Momsen played the daughter. She had straight brown hair parted down the middle and wore no make-up. Times have changed for her.

I could go on, but frankly, I don't remember the names of half of them and it just makes me depressed thinking about all the hours I spent working on shows that never saw the light of day. Pilots that don't get picked up are as heartbreaking for the casting director they are for the actors. We give up so much of our personal lives during the casting process, it's ridiculous that we keep doing them. It's also ridiculous how much money the networks are willing to spend on projects that never air.

I spent one pilot season in the NBC executive offices as manager of casting. I oversaw the casting of many pilots and was in the network test as an executive (not as the casting director or associate of any one project, which was my usual role). During that pilot season, I oversaw the casting of *Medium* and *The Office*. Also during that pilot season was a show called *D.O.T.S.* (Department of Transportation Services). It was about meter maids. I thought it was hilarious, but it was really more of a Fox show. We did have to fire and replace two of the actors after the first day of rehearsal. Never a good time.

As of this writing (2019), pilot season is so truncated as to render it unrecognizable. The networks—who where the only game in town for decades—have become dinosaurs, and most folks in the industry wonder how much longer they will be around, at least as we knew them. This last pilot season saw a significant drop in how many pilots were produced and an even more significant drop in how many were picked up to go to series —the average was 3 per network.

Cable and streaming services such as Hulu, Netflix and Amazon don't create pilots in the traditional sense. Most of their shows are "straight to series." The exceptions are Disney and Nickelodeon.

146

The casting process for series regulars for a straight-to-series order is pretty much the same as what the networks do, but they are done as-needed, all-year-round, thus eliminating "pilot season" as we know it. Be skeptical of workshops and such "preparing you for pilot season." These are usually held in the winter. You should be preparing for pilot season all year round by getting out in the world and doing all the many things this book discusses.

Also, as I claimed in the first chapter, please be aware of people using the term "pilot" loosely. It can sometimes be bandied about by folks trying to appear more important than they are or to elevate the status of a project that is nothing more than a self-produced spec project.

A true pilot is the first episode of a prospective television show that is *already attached to a network and studio* and for which and that the network is paying the tab. What it *isn't* is a self- or crowdfunded short video which the creator has hopes of selling to a network, cable channel or a streaming service. "It's being shopped around" means there is no network or studio attached and it might never get made and you might never get paid. It also means that it is not the time to boast on Facebook that you booked a pilot.

One is more likely to win the lottery than to sell a spec pilot to a network, cable channel or streaming service.

For the most part, the networks are in development with writer-producers who already have a track record of writing for shows that have been on the air. There is so much money involved in financing a television show these days that a network is unlikely to take a chance on an unknown. Netflix, the renegade, is really no different; same with Hulu originals. And prestige cable channels like HBO, Showtime, Starz, are Fort Knox as well.

If you are ever asked to audition for a "pilot," please get all the facts before proceeding. The best place to look is on the breakdown. If there is no breakdown as described above…well…that's your first red flag.

10 THE WELL-ROUNDED ACTOR

Now, more than ever, the only way for an actor to make a living at acting is to have the agility to work in network TV, cable, streaming formats, film, commercials, new media, and theatre. In order to give up your day job and make your income solely on acting, you have to be good at auditioning for all media. In order to feed your soul, you have to be able to do plays. Performing in plays affords an actor the opportunity to collaborate on an artistic endeavor that is stimulating, intellectual, emotional, and physical.

I'm biased toward well-trained theatre actors. Although I enjoy actors like Seth Rogen and admire Jonah Hill (who, by the way is amazing in the audition room), I get most excited by those actors whose background is in traditional theatre and musicals. I believe that theatre training is the best foundation for an actor. It allows a safe place for actors to learn who they are as performers. It's where an actor learns how to analyze a script and how to break down a character. It provides the actor with technique and a working knowledge of Constantin Stanislavski's teachings—"The Method"—as well as those of Michael Chekhov, Sanford Meisner, and all the other great acting teachers of the past. Voice and movement classes are also essential to the actor's craft. The theatre offers an actor discipline and knowledge beyond acting.

So many great TV actors come from theatre; Laurie Metcalf, Christine Baranski, Jesse Tyler Ferguson, Bellamy Young, Michael Emerson, Bryan Cranston, Josh Radnor, and to some extent Neil Patrick Harris, who started as a kid on a TV show but has since juggled his on-camera work with musical theatre (*Assassins, Company, Hedwig and the Angry Inch*).

One of the many joys of working on *Frasier* was that all the writer-producers on that show truly appreciated good theatre actors. David Hyde

Pierce, John Mahoney, and Kelsey Grammer all come from the theatre. On the show, we stole from the Los Angeles, New York and London stages all the time: Sir Derek Jacobi (playing a terrible Shakespearian actor), Nathan Lane, Brian Stokes Mitchell, Carolee Carmello, Jean Smart and Harriet Sansom Harris, to name only a few. They were all brilliant and could handle with ease the erudite and witty language of the show.

In some circles, there is a bias *against* theatre and theatre training. When I taught Acting and Directing for the Camera at University of Colorado, Boulder, where we brought together twenty filmmakers from the film studies department and twenty actors from the theatre department, I could feel the initial unspoken tension between the theatre and film students. It wasn't true for them all, but there was enough to make it uncomfortable. The actors didn't think the filmmakers knew how to talk to actors and the filmmakers thought the actors were "too theatrical." All too often, people get lumped into stereotyped categories, and for some odd reason, those who love and study theatre experience the worst of it.

Describing an actor as being "too theatrical" is a derogatory blanket statement. What does it mean? If it's meant to say that the actor is not authentic, I'm here to tell you that any actor, whether they do plays or have never stepped foot on a stage, can be inauthentic. I hate that the theatre stigma is applied so broadly and blindly to all theatre trained actors.

Kelsey Grammer, who is a trained theatre actor, is not subtle. In fact, some might call him "theatrical," but he has great depth, so it never seems like he is overacting. He won many Emmy® Awards for being larger than life. The same can be said about John Lithgow, Sean Hayes, and Glenn Close. If another actor who has no depth were to try doing what they do, it would be unbearable to watch.

I prefer to use the term *calibration,* like the fader on a sound board. Actors have to find their own calibration for camera work, whether they're theatre actors or not. On-camera work, especially with dramatic film and episodic shows, is all about the eyes. All the energy you might put into your whole body on stage now must all be focused in your eyes. It is through the eyes that we see into you. Seeing your thoughts moves us.

A common misconception theatre actors have confuses being more natural with doing nothing. They fear being "too big" and so tone down so much that they literally have nothing going on in their eyes and can appear robotic. Doing too much and doing too little are equally ineffective. Each actor has to find the perfect balance where he or she is natural, real, and showing the full range of human emotion in their eyes. If you follow the precepts of charisma discussed earlier—being relaxed, showing vulnerability, showing your true self, being a good listener, revealing your natural sexiness, etc.—then you will find your on-camera self. You will discover your individual calibration. You will be wonderful, we will fall in love with you, and you will book jobs.

It's shortsighted and unrealistic to come into this business with the goal of being just a movie actor. Practically speaking, it's far more difficult to get cast in a film than in any other medium. Even though it seems that everyone and their mother is making a movie these days, there are fewer films than ever before being produced in the traditional studio system, where actors are paid a union wage. And even in a studio film, only the stars get paid a substantial amount of money; all the other actors in the roster get paid "scale plus ten percent," dependent on which SAG-AFTRA contract is being used on the film. And the contract depends on the budget of the film. Scale, which is the contractual minimum amount an actor can be paid, could be $900 a day, it could be $125 a day.

In the case of the "ultra low budget" films that are currently all the rage, the actor's salary is often "deferred," which means an actor won't get paid if the film never finds distribution. Most indie films never get finished let alone get distributed. For every *Paranormal Activity* or *Madeline's Madeline,* there are thousands of films out there being made in every burg and every corner of the globe that never see the light of day.

Just as an actor can't make a living just being in movies, an actor can't make a living just being a regional theatre actor. Maybe with the exception of the Oregon Shakespeare Festival in Ashland, the days of an actor being a company member—employed full-time, all season long by a prestigious theatre company (such as Steppenwolf in Chicago or South Coast Repertory in Southern California)—are long gone. I know some exceptional actors who have devoted their entire careers to the regional theatre system and are now in their 50s or older. Most feel that they have nothing to show for all their hard work. They have little or no film for posterity, and they don't have the amount of money that their successful colleagues in film and episodic have at this point in their lives. They also lack the network and prestige streaming credits that can get them into the audition rooms. In the worst cases, theatre actors have had to either leave the business entirely or take on menial side jobs to make ends meet. Alas, I know many brilliant actors in this category. I suppose this is the plight of any true artist living in America—living hand-to-mouth just to be able to do what you love. Perhaps that's a discussion for another book.

What this book is about, of course, is how to make a living as an actor, and the bread and butter of any working actor's life in today's marketplace are episodic roles. There are more roles available in this medium than any other. Major film stars have worked in TV—Will Smith, Tom Hanks, Denzel Washington, George Clooney, Shia LaBeouf (who was on the Disney Channel's *Even Stevens),* and Ryan Gosling, who was a Mouseketeer. If there ever was a stigma against a film actor doing episodic, it no longer exists. Nicole Kidman and Reese Witherspoon are doing episodic for goodness sake. In fact, for some it's preferred because the shooting schedule is so much easier than back-to-back studio films.

An actor needs to be able to do it all to keep working. Allison Janney's career is a prime example of the well-rounded career I'm talking about. This award-winning actress is a theatre trained actor who has appeared on Broadway (*A View From The Bridge, Present Laughter, 9 to 5, Six Degrees of Separation*), soap operas *(Guiding Light)*, multi-cam sitcoms *(Mom)*, hour dramas *(West Wing)*, single-camera comedies *(Mr. Sunshine)*, independent films *(Juno, I Tanya)*, studio films *(The Help)*, and is the voice of Kaiser Permanente in their commercials. She's not easy to typecast and as a young actress she was told her height (6') was a detriment. She has been quoted as saying, "Years ago, one casting agent told me that the only roles I could play were lesbians and aliens."

Adam Driver, who is probably the unlikeliest leading man in the traditional sense, made a big splash in New York City theater not playing the lead. In Broadways shows such as *Look Back in Anger* in which he played a supporting role, his charisma and fierceness on stage was undeniable. He went on to do HBO's *Girls* and is now a major film star; yet he returns to the Broadway stage whenever he can *(Burn This)*.

The bottom line is, in order to make a living, you have to do it all, or at least try and master more than three of these outlets—network TV, cable, streaming, web series (that pay), feature films, theater, commercials, print, industrials, hosting, being a spokesperson, leading focus groups and promotional events, voice over, audio books, role-playing for job-training services... the list is probably endless.

11 FINAL WORDS 3.0

I have spent twenty-four years—and still counting—as a casting director. Although I'm doing other things now—writing, directing theater, producing, coaching, public speaking and reading from my own stories at spoken word events—I still consider myself a casting director and I always view actors through that lens. There are times when it is heartbreaking and there are times when magic happens. Despite the time I've spent feeling frustrated or bored out of my mind, there have been more times in which I got goose bumps and was emotionally moved. I laughed, I cried, I helped thousands of actors pursue their passion and hundreds of directors and writers see their projects come to life.

Still, I sometimes ask what it's all *for*. Are the costs, compromises, and countless hours spent all worth it? As I wrote above, there is a large cost that your family ends up paying for you to pursue your passion, and my daughter, Kate, paid a high price.

As with many endeavors, it was multifaceted, complex…"it was the best of times and it was the worst of times." I have a great life, a privileged life. I'm not digging ditches. I am so grateful for all that has happened to me, the good and the not-so-good.

Fulfilling your wildest dreams will not change the facts of your childhood. It never brought my dad back to life and it won't make your family less dysfunctional.

If you become desperate and needy, thinking that you'll never book jobs and envious of actors who do, it's time to get out of the business. The casting directors will smell your self-defeat a mile away and will not hire you.

Please have sympathy for the casting directors. We get as nervous as you do. We are under more pressure and stress than you can imagine. Remember to always make it about the other person and make the audition about us and not you.

Why is it that some actors become very successful and others do not? What do you do if you have insurmountable obstacles to overcome? What if you're very talented but crippled with insecurity? What exactly do you do with the information if you're told you're too tall or that you're too old to get an agent? What if someone thinks your calves are too big (actresses have actually been told that) or, like Alison Janney, that you are too tall? The reality is that any and all actors have limitations. Very few actors and actresses are the embodiment of some human physical ideal. Regardless of skin color, shape of eye, weight, or sexual orientation; and in spite of the world's prejudices and biases; it's *your* job to change our minds. In order to get work, you will have to shake up preconceived notions of how certain characters are to be portrayed.

If you're confused at all about where you fit in, instead of wondering what type you are, I would suggest you start a list of actors who are taking your roles. Watch movies and episodic shows and start taking note of the actors who are in the roles you might be right for. Be honest with yourself; you might admire Rachel McAdams, but is she taking your roles? You might, instead, be more like an Aubrey Plaza. We need as many Aubrey Plazas as we do Rachel McAdamses.

Advances in camera technology have altered considerably the kinds of people we see on the small and big screens. When the predominant format went from film to video, and cameras became smaller and easier to use, a huge shift in styles happened in the way TV shows and films look and feel. Feature films no longer have to look glamorous and slick, and episodic shows have become more like documentaries. With the proliferation of the hand-held style of filmmaking ("shaky cam") made mainstream by mockumentary shows such as *The Office* or films like *Paranormal Activity*, a more naturalistic style of acting has come into demand and the types of actors populating these more "real" worlds are more "normal" looking. Episodic and films, for the most part, are as much a reflection of the world we actually live as they are of the world we desire.

In 2009 I wrote that "the two basic types are leading and character. You are either a leading or a character actor." I stated that "if you're an ingenue, then you must be comfortable with the unspoken rules related to weight, body type, ethnicity, and beauty. If you're a leading man, you have to seem straight, be incredibly sexy yet vulnerable, and be typically handsome. TV shows and films are all about sex, after all, and every show and film must have an object of desire."

Thank God this is no longer true. It used to be that objects of desire had to fit a certain traditional mold. When I first started in casting, the cookie-cutter female roles as exemplified in *Friends,* etc.— actresses who were size zero and white—dominated the landscape. But *no more!*

The bottom line is that, more than ever, there is now an opportunity for all types of actors to find good roles. You absolutely do not have to audition trying to be someone you're not. You don't have to change a thing. Just come in as yourself, quirks and all. In fact, the quirkier the better.

In 2012, I wrote "My wish for the third edition of this book is that I'll be writing about the *overabundance* of diverse actors on TV. I hope that one day soon the faces I see on the small and big screens will reflect in equal amounts the mix of people I see in American sports, the music industry, and just plain walking around in my world." I'm ecstatic to be able to write now in 2019 that my wish came true.

There is a lot of information about the acting profession available to you out there. You will get a lot of opinions and advice thrown your way, some contradicting the opinions you most cherish. All I can tell you is always be wise, go with your gut, and Google and IMDb everyone you meet who offers you something, especially if they want you to take their class or workshop. Don't reach out to agents and managers blindly. Do your research. If they reach out to you first, beware.

Don't do anything with anybody without checking their credits on IMDb first. Do they reflect the high standards that you want to attain?

You must master auditioning. Auditioning is like being in the finals at Wimbledon. You can't blow a single point. You have to be in your zone and hit every single ball with all that you have in you.

You must know who you are—the dark side as well as the light— and be comfortable with all aspects of your personality. You can't be someone you're not, even if you have buckets of money to spend on plastic surgery. You have to be genuine and believable. Being a great actor is not about pretense (ironic, isn't it?). So many people go into acting because they love to pretend they're someone else. In reality, those who succeed are able to reveal who they already are—the good, the bad, and the ugly.

If you cannot look in the mirror without cringing, or can't bear being by yourself for even a whole day, don't go into acting. Acting is facing who you are all of the time.

You must possess a life force. If you don't have passion, desire, and charisma, why should we spend time auditioning you? Being in the room with an actor who has no charisma is demoralizing to us. We can't be emotionally moved by an actor who is not passionate.

With charisma, you eventually will succeed, even if your calves are big or you're too old to get an agent. Charisma trumps height, old age, and bad teeth. Look at Alison Janney, Kathy Joosten (RIP), and John C. Reilly.

You are all the casting director has. We don't write the scripts, we don't design the sets, all we do is find actors. You are the sole reflection of all our hard work and passion. So, when you get the precious opportunity to audition, remember that and make us all look brilliant. We love you, you know.

TOP TEN SECRETS OF CHARISMA—A RECAP

1) **Reveal your natural sexiness and you'll own the room.** There is nothing like looking into your lover's face and seeing his or her eyes look at you in "that way." They are open, relaxed, reflecting a positive energy and desire. We can't help but be drawn into that. If you can convey your natural sexiness without being gross about it, you will own us. Your natural sexiness is the true you in a relaxed state. Try flirting with your audience. Look at them with love, not fear.

2) **Create chemistry in the audition room by making it about the other person.** You don't want to be a selfish lover, so don't be a selfish actor. Whatever you have to say should be about the other person—either the other character in the scene or your audience in the room. That is why you're there in the first place— what is your relationship to them? How do you feel about them? What do you want from them? It's the chemistry that happens between people that creates magic.

3) **Express vulnerability to exude magnetism.** The more we can see your vulnerability, your humanness, your reflection of the human condition, the more we are drawn to you. Good actors are brave folks. They go emotionally where others are afraid to. That's why we want to watch them so much. Good leaders have the same quality. Is your public persona different from your private persona? Try showing more sadness, more fear, more genuine humor in your public side.

4) **Control the adrenaline rush to increase your personal power.** It's your job to make your audience comfortable so they can enjoy and listen to what you have to say. If you're nervous, we'll feel

162

sorry for you, we will feel compassion, but we won't be moved to take action. Some ways to combat nerves: yoga, meditation, hypnotherapy (www.stephanie-jones.com).

5) **All we want is you.** It doesn't matter how cute you are or who you know—if your audience can't connect to you as a person, they won't be interested. If you're a different person in your audition than you are when you initially walked in the room, the you who walked in the room will be the one we want to connect with. Are you emotionally blocked, not being genuine?

6) **Be a good listener and connect with your audience powerfully.** The first rule of dating and relationships is that it's the communication between people that moves us. Are you talking *at* us or simply talking *to* us? Stop thinking about how you're doing and just be present.

7) **Show humility to create lasting relationships.** Be confident, not arrogant—there is a huge difference. Confidence is when you're sure of yourself, when you feel comfortable in your own skin. Arrogance is when you don't feel sure of yourself, but you're acting as if you do. In acting as in dating, arrogance is one of the biggest turn-offs there is. And actors who are slick and "act" make us want to run out of the room.

8) **In order to avoid self-consciousness, don't think so much.** If you start analyzing your work as you're doing it, you will kill the spontaneity. Your audience can tell when you're not present in the moment and are preoccupied. Good preparation and feeling good about what you're doing are the keys to conquering your self-consciousness, along with just being comfortable in your own skin. Maybe a good improvisation class would be good for you. It works with actors who are "too tight."

163

9) **Don't try so hard in the audition or self-tape, just be.** Try too hard to make us like you and you'll turn us away. Try too hard to be good, and you'll just get tired. Great athletes make it look easy. There has to be an ease in everything you do, otherwise you will make your audience uncomfortable. If you've ever seen wannabe comic actors trying to be funny in order to get on a sitcom, you'll know what I mean. There's a desperation there that is not pretty.

10) **Be healthy emotionally and physically and be a hero.** In order to be around for the long haul, you must be healthy in every way. The ideal actor is the ideal person. Your audience looks up to you; they admire you. You are the representative of humanity. You have a great responsibility. Eat right, exercise, and go to therapy! Don't make the excuse you don't have time. You won't have time if you don't do these things.

Things I Learned Doing Standup for the First Time

1) I admire performers of any kind even more than I already did, which was a lot. You truly are brave souls, revealing your dark and light in order to share stories. It's a very raw experience.

2) Stories are exciting. Others want to hear what you're about. What's your POV. Where do you come from. Sharing in an authentic is the connectivity we all need.

3) Don't let the one hate cancel out all of the oceans of love. You put yourself out there in a public way, especially if you post the video on social media, so you're bound to get some hate. But actually getting it is so shitty it makes you want to crawl into a hole and never do it again. But I did get a lot of love, and that's been fantastic primarily cause you are connecting with others and that's really the reason for living.

4) I need to finally get over feeling self-conscious about myself and how I look. Dogged me my whole life. Let's be rid of this shackle, shall we?

5) Telling funny stories is a lot more fun than telling sad ones. If you can take your sad stories and make them funny, in a good way, that is enlightening to others. It makes you feel you can truly #changethemovieschangetheworld I'm feeling that way right now.

I will do it again. And maybe many more times. It's such a good outlet for me. And makes me an even better teacher and casting director and general lover of the performing arts.

(January 23, 2016—Los Angeles)

4 Things You Need to Know About CDs

Casting Directors have been around officially since the late '60s–early '70s. There's a superb film—*Casting By*—that covers those early years very well (when American Broadway actors would be found for films instead of the other way around, as it is today). It's been said we have the "keys to the kingdom," and you have to get our approval before you can truly begin to "achieve your dreams."

I've been a CD for 20 years now. Jeff Greenberg (*Frasier, Modern Family*) gave me my big break and helped me achieve my dreams. I've been in the *inner sanctum* known as network episodic (before Cable as we know it) and I've struggled to make ends meet working in New Media. I truly have seen it all… and I'm here to tell you, we are human.

1) **We Love Actors.** Period. We grew up watching non-stop episodic, film, and some of us, like me, theater as well. We were not the most popular kids. We never dreamed we'd have a job as cool as this one… because we are star struck and love actors. Actors have given us a gift— we can get lost in their emotions and experiences when they perform. You help us by feeling and doing things we can't. Crying or laughing in the dark, as part of an audience, is one of favorite things.

2) **We Are Not Acting Teachers.** Although some of us do teach and coach actors, when we are a casting director in the room or watching self-tapes/demos, we have to find the best actors and, especially for episodic, we have to find them friggin' *fast*. If we had all the time, energy, and stamina in the world, we could spend at least 20 minutes on each actor who comes in, redirecting and such, making them a better performer, but we don't, so we go with our gut. For those of us who've been doing this a long time, our gut is damn good at sniffing out wanna-bes and moving on—also good at spotting true talent.

3) **We Are Not Your Adversaries.** Don't be intimidated by us. We *want* to connect with you, yes even when we might seem distracted and not look up as much as you would like. *We have a lot on our minds.* The whole project rests on our already weary shoulders. Sometimes we can hide that pressure and stress from you, sometimes we can't. But we

always want you to be The One. Please be together and brilliant. That's all we ask.

4) **We Have Lives.** If we would watch every demo that comes our way or attend everything we're invited to, we'd *never* eat, do laundry, take care of kids or see our friends, mates, or families. We wouldn't take good care of *ourselves* (which, alas, is what happened to me.) Slow down with the postcards (which we don't keep), links, newsletters, invitations. Just do the work, and if you're great, we'll find you.

Thanks for listening.

(November 8, 2014—Los Angeles)

Discover Yourself

Before you can be discovered by a casting director, you must discover yourself.

I know this not only because I'm a casting director but because I wanted desperately to be an actress when I was young. Unfortunately, I also wanted desperately to be someone else. These two desires cancelled each other out.

We're not looking for an "image." As Alex Loyd says in his terrific self-help book, The Healing Code (www.thehealingcode.com), the erroneous precept that "image is everything" originates from the belief that "I'm not okay, and if people get to know me, they will come to that same conclusion, so whatever the cost I need people to see a manufactured me instead of who I really am." Portraying yourself in an inauthentic, pre-packaged way is manipulation in the worst way and we can see right through that.

In truth, you can wow us by simply being yourself. This is true in all auditioning, but especially for episodic roles. All we want is you, and to see your authentic, natural charisma coming through the character.

I've come to realize, because of all the hours I've spent in that room, that the key ingredients to the Art of Charisma are self-knowledge (with self-acceptance) and balance. In order to tap into the full power of your individual charisma, you absolutely must know who you are and then have the ability to reveal that true self in the room or on a self-tape. If you aren't brave enough to look deep within in order to truly know and accept who you are, then you most likely won't be a very good actor.

Your true self is a reflection of both your dark and light qualities. A charismatic person is the perfect balance of the two. If you are all dark qualities, you will scare us, and if you are all light qualities, we won't be emotionally moved by you. Shakespeare's plays are all about self-knowledge and balance. If you're too much of one thing, you either end up dead or your family is destroyed (Macbeth, King Lear). If you're the perfect balance of man and woman, dark and light, you end up happily married (Rosalind in As You Like It).

So you must ask yourself, with honesty and fearlessness, "Who am I? What emotional qualities do I possess?" As an actor, the only thing you can play is emotions. It's the only thing the audience responds to, really. You think we're attracted to hot bodies? No. We're attracted to a strong emotional inner life that is your emotional inner life and not someone you are trying to be.

(August 30, 2014 - Los Angeles)

170

What Does "Too Theatrical" Even Mean???

My mission is to help strong, well-trained actors make the transition from theater to film/episodic/commercials, while still respecting and cherishing their work on the stage. A well-rounded actor is Golden.

Now, more than ever, the only way for an actor to make a living at acting is to have the agility to work in episodic, film, commercials, new media, and theatre. In order to give up your day job and make your income solely on acting, you have to be good at auditioning for all media. In order to feed your soul, you have to be able to do plays. Performing in plays affords an actor the opportunity to collaborate on an artistic endeavor that is stimulating, intellectual, emotional, and physical."

In some circles, there is a bias against theatre and theatre training. When I taught "Acting and Directing for the Camera" at University of Colorado, Boulder, where we brought together twenty filmmakers from the film studies department and twenty actors from the theatre department, I could feel the initial unspoken tension between the theatre and film students. Not with all the students but enough to make it uncomfortable. The actors didn't think the filmmakers knew how to talk to actors and the filmmakers thought the actors were "too theatrical." All too often, people get lumped into stereotyped categories, and for some odd reason, those who love and study theatre experience the worst of it.

Describing an actor as being "too theatrical" means that the actor is not authentic, and any actor, whether they do plays or have never stepped foot on a stage, can be inauthentic. I hate that the theatre stigma is bandied about so broadly and applied blindly to all theatre trained actors.

Actors have to find their own calibration for camera work, whether they're theatre actors or not. On-camera work, especially with dramatic film and episodic shows, is all about the eyes. All the energy you might put into your whole body on stage now must all be focused in your eyes. It is through the eyes that we see into you. Seeing your thoughts moves us.

A common misconception younger theatre actors have, however, confuses being more natural with doing nothing. Some tone down so much that they literally have nothing going on in their eyes and can appear robotic. Doing too much and doing too little are equally ineffective. Each actor has to find the perfect balance where he or she is natural, real, and showing the full range of human emotion reflected in the eyes. If you follow the precepts of charisma discussed earlier—being relaxed, showing vulnerability, showing your true self, being a good listener, revealing your natural sexiness, etc.—then you will find your on-camera self. You will be wonderful, we will fall in love with you, and you will book jobs.

(July 10, 2014 - Los Angeles)

172

3 Tips for Nailing Single-Camera Comedy Auditions

Each genre of episodic and film requires different styles of auditioning. This column will be about single-camera comedies. I'm extremely fortunate to have been given the opportunity to work on an Emmy-winning multi-cam sitcom *(Frasier)* and a single-camera comedy *(Arrested Development)*. When I look back, it seems like a dream. I wish I would have appreciated my experiences more while they were happening, but such is life, I suppose. You don't know what you've got 'til it's gone. *Arrested Development* is now like the granddaddy of the modern single-cameras.

Single-camera comedies are shot in five days, but unlike multi-cams, they're shot like short indie films and usually directed by the hottest indie film directors. They endure hectic shoot schedules with long days and no time for rehearsal. They are shot out of sequence, as all films are, and it's easy to get lost in the mayhem. You most likely will not get too many notes from the director if you get any at all. But first, you have to do extremely well in the audition.

1. **Embrace short scenes.** The sides you will be asked to prepare for this type of show are short and staccato-like. They are not like scenes from a play, or even from a sitcom, where there is a normal exchange between one or more people with some momentum within the scene. There is usually no beginning, middle, or end to the scene, which might be only five-lines long. Remember, Justin Grant Wade (Steve Holt on *Arrested Development)* only had two words at his audition! The comedy in the single-camera show is in the style and the situation, not in the jokes. Hilarious inserts and quick cuts, juxtaposing one scene with the next, elevate the humor but have nothing to do with acting. You will not be the setup of a joke that the star will deliver. The language is not witty. You might have one line here and one line on the next page, with a silent bit at the end of the scene in reaction to what the star has just said or done in the situation. You can find humor in the silent reaction to what the other characters are saying. You can find humor in just a look or in the quality you bring into the audition—the non-verbals.

2. **Don't get lost in your sides.** Because the non-verbals are so important in these auditions, it's all the more essential that you don't have your nose in the sides during the audition. Obvious, I know, but if we can't see your eyes, we can't see your reaction. The humor is found in the thought processes you reveal and not so much in what you say. But because you might have one line (or more likely one word) on one page and then another line on the next page, you can't be looking down in order to keep your place in the scene. Acting is reacting, right? All the more important in this kind of comedy. You must be so prepared with the material that it's second nature to you and yet spontaneous. A good general rule of thumb: Always be connected to the person you're doing the scene with, whether it be a reader, another actor, or directly into the camera a la "Parks and Recreation." If you're truly connected, we will not only see your reaction in your eyes, but the scene will have an emotional life—an urgency.

3. **Don't try to be funny.** Although Aubrey Plaza, Tony Hale, and Rainn Wilson are hilariously funny, they achieve the humor by revealing their own quirky selves. The roles are meant to be funny in an idiosyncratic way. You need to bring your own individual idiosyncratic self into the audition without trying to be funny. Trying to be anything means you are working way too hard. You just have to be. The comedy needs to be played with great subtlety. Go watch Mae Whitman and Judy Greer in old *Arrested Development* episodes if you want to learn from the masters of the guest star roles in one-camera comedies.

(Reposted from *Backstage* where I had a weekly column)

(July 24, 2014 - Los Angeles)

3 Tips for Nailing Multi-Camera Sitcom Auditions

Each genre of episodic and film requires different styles of auditioning. This column will be one of several in a series and first up is multi-camera sitcoms. When I first cut my teeth on sitcoms, *Frasier*, "Friends," and "Seinfeld" were the norm and not the oddity on network episodic that they are now. I learned from the bes—Jeff Greenberg and all the writer-producers who ran *Frasier*— and quickly discovered that actors who trained in theater had the discipline and inherent theatricality best served on these shows.

Multi-camera sitcoms rehearse for four days, teching and shooting on the fifth day in front of a live audience. Current network shows in this genre are "2 Broke Girls," "The Big Bang Theory," and "Last Man Standing." Cable channels such as episodic Land, Disney, and TBS are where most of the sitcoms now broadcast ("Hot in Cleveland," "Jessie," "Sullivan & Son").

Here are three things to keep in mind when auditioning for multi-camera sitcoms.

1. **Energy level is heightened naturalism.** Since multi-cams are most like plays, the energy necessary to "pop" in these auditions are brighter than normal, but not so big that you are overacting and/or trying to be "funny." This is not sketch comedy a la "SNL," where the characters are over the top to the point of absurdity. You audition with a heightened version of yourself that is carefully calibrated while seeming spontaneous. If you are naturally neurotic, you can bump up your neurosis. If you are optimistic or happy, you would bump up your perkiness. Whatever traits you have in your real life, you can use those in creating the character you bring in—your comic persona that is discovered and refined as explained in a previous column.

I was witness to countless auditions in which actors would try to make their auditions unique by adding an accent or creating a larger-than-life character that was a caricature. Some actors used strange gestures in order to make the material funnier. Some wore funny glasses or a funny tie. These tactics always flopped.

175

2. **Stick to the words.** This is true for multi-cams more than with any other genre. The writer-producers run the show in episodic, remember, so when you mess with their words, especially with multi-cams, they will not hire you. The writers of multi-cams harbor over the creation of each phrase, figuring out which word to place at the end of a sentence to make the line funnier. If you add extraneous "ahhs," "ums," or "you knows," you will destroy the rhythm of the line. You cannot invert a line or change the syntax or punctuation of the line. If you do so, you will sabotage the delivery the writers painstakingly labored to achieve. Think of it as witty repartee in a Noël Coward play. You would not paraphrase Coward's lines. You would not paraphrase Shakespeare's lines. It is all about rhythm and comic timing. The timing is quick and witty, like the dialogue in a Woody Allen comedy. You cannot take too much time within the scene. Once it slows down, you will kill the energy and the quick-witted pace. The lines need to overlap each other, like a funny conversation in real life.

If, in those rare cases, the writer-producer wants you to improvise, either they or the casting director will let you know usually before the audition begins. If they say nothing, assume they want you to say their words exactly as written…and save your excellent improv skills for the single-camera comedies.

3. **Remain focused and calm in moments of stress.** Since multi-cams are performed in front of a live audience, the writer-producer needs to feel in the audition room (or on the tape) that you are smart on your feet and confident in your skills. It is like doing a play, but without the six weeks of rehearsal prior to opening. The writer-producers can and will change the lines as they see fit at anytime during the process, whether it be right before a run-through or during the shoot, and you will have to go with the flow with ease and a positive attitude. The last thing the writer-producers want to worry about is an actor—especially one who is a guest just for the week. More than likely you will be working on a show that is a well-oiled machine and you don't want to slow down the process in any way, whether it be asking too many questions or messing up the lines. You can't be too casual on the set with the rest of the cast just because the series regulars are acting like it's no big deal. They're under contract, secure in their jobs on the show, and often won't know their lines until the day of the shoot. You are a visitor in their world. You must be a perfect

person and know your lines, even when they change constantly. You must not challenge the director or be too friendly with the stars.

Actors must be graceful under pressure…and naturally funny as well.

(Reposted from *Backstage* where I had a weekly column)

(August 15, 2014 - Los Angeles)

5 Ways to Remain Enthusiastic

I love *Mad Men,* and one of my favorite quotes from that show is said to Don Draper by an ex-lover. "I hope she knows, you only like the beginnings of things."

Similarly, it's easy to be enthusiastic about acting when you are first getting started, but how can you avoid feeling jaded and bitter down the road? When you lose your enthusiasm, you lose everything. Here are some ideas to keep it going.

1. Watch well-made film and television. Do it just for the *enjoyment* of it. Remember when you were very young and you just couldn't wait to watch your favorite program on episodic or go to a movie theater on the opening weekend of the film you waited months to see? Sometimes when you've been in the Industry too long, you forget about the love that brought you there in the first place. Just as with a long marriage, it's good to rekindle that love. And when you *do* watch something and you keep saying, "I could do better than *that* actor," it might be time to take a long break and reconsider your goals. Envy and frustration are not great traits to have as an actor. They will eat you up inside, and we need you to stay positive.

2. Have hobbies not related to the business. This is the toughest aspect for me. My hobbies are watching episodic and films. I enjoy watching movies in a movie theater more than anything. This is not healthy. Acquiring outside interests, such as gardening, fitness, baseball, etc., will help take your mind off your troubles when the going gets tough…and the going will get tough.

3. Have a place of worship. Be it a mosque, church, synagogue, yoga center, temple, what have you, you will live more enthusiastically if you belong to a community of folks who believe in more than just the self. If you don't communicate with a positive entity greater than yourself, you will get lost. I've tried it. It doesn't work.

4. Seek therapy in hard times. When you become despondent, hopeless, feeling like you want to quit the business and run away from your life, and these feelings last more than a week, seek therapy. Being in therapy is not a sign of weakness, it's a sign of great strength. Asking for help is the hardest thing one can do, but it must be done if you are trying to sustain a positive outlook. Believe me, you'll feel better immediately. And you can't use lack of funds as an excuse, as there are good options for therapy even for low-income individuals.

5. Don't let your angst get in the way of feeling joy. Being an artist of any kind is a two-sided coin. On one side, we experience feelings of angst, pain, and worthlessness usually coupled with a large ego. These feelings can be positive as they help us be sensitive and compassionate towards our fellow human beings. The other side—the light side—is optimism, hope, and joy. As with everything essential for our survival, balance is the key, and when our dark side is out of whack, enthusiasm gets drowned out. Don't let this happen to you.

(Reposted from *Backstage* where I had a weekly column)

(September 19, 2014 - Los Angeles)

Defining and Refining Your Comic Persona

Mindy Kaling, Zooey Deschanel, Rainn Wilson, Andy Samberg, Jim Parsons, Josh Radnor, Charlyne Yi, Aubrey Plaza, Stephanie Beatriz, Joel McHale, Jesse Tyler Ferguson, Ken Jeong, and of course, Amy Poehler and Tiny Fey—these are but a few of the wonderful comic actors we love who are populating the television landscape. They are all very distinct, with their own comic personas they refined coming up the ranks in either theater (Ferguson, Deschanel, Beatriz, Wilson, Parsons, Radnor, McHale), improv/sketch (Samberg, Yi, Poehler, Fey, Jeong), or both (Kaling). For the most part, they are the same in every role they have played, with the same quirks, delivery, timing, and sensibility, and we don't want them to change a thing because we *love* them, just the way they are. They are all endearing, relatable, hilarious, and have enviable careers, and so can you.

How can you create and refine a comic persona that you can use over and over again in every audition, for every role, whether it be for a multi-camera sitcom, one-camera comedy, Web series, or sketch/improv show? First and foremost, you have to know who *you* are. You can't refine who you are if you are always trying to be someone you are not, thinking that's the way to get others to like you. In the audition room, you can't give us what *we* want, you have to give us *you,* at your core and a bit heightened. If you are not naturally deadpan—you can't do what Aubrey Plaza does (and so brilliantly)—it will come off as fake and actor-y.

Zooey Deschanel is the queen of the "quirky girl," a type that is so popular now. How she is on "New Girl" (or was in "Elf" or "(500) Days of Summer"), was who she was as "Little Red Riding Hood" in an Equity-waiver production of "Into the Woods" in The Valley, which I had the great pleasure of seeing her in when she was 12. Even then, she was dorky, all-knowing, a little bit sad and uncertain, and incredibly confident and commanding of who she was…even at that young age.

Who are *you*? You must answer this question with honesty and fearlessness. What emotional qualities do you possess? As an actor, the only things you can play are emotions, as they are what we respond to. You think we're attracted to hot bodies? We're not. We're attracted to a strong emotional inner life that reveals to us who you truly are, both dark and light, and that you *own* without any apologies or pretense. Try a simple exercise: Make a list of at least 10 *emotional* qualities you possess. Are you sad, angry, optimistic, fierce, funny, smart, insecure, and confident? The great thing about emotional qualities is that they can be contradictory, and in fact, they help create the best comic personas—an everyman at odds with himself. Mindy Kaling is sexy, goofy, confident, and insecure.

Once you know who you are, then get out there and practice your comic persona, whether it's in an improv class or show, open mics, and/or a Web series of your own creation. Refinement doesn't come overnight, it takes a lot of work, discovery, insight, fearlessness, and a damn good sense of humor—*your* humor.

(Reposted from *Backstage* where I had a weekly column)

(October 5, 2014 - Los Angeles)

4 Free Things an Actor Can Do To Improve

It seems that everywhere an actor turns, he or she is required to spend money—classes, headshots, workshops, wardrobe, books (including mine), etc. Here are a few ideas for ways you can practice your craft without spending any money.*

(*Predicated on the fact you read my first column in *Backstage* and already have a video camera of some sort and the capability of being online.)

1. Tape yourself every day. Just as an athlete has to workout every day, a writer has to write every day, and a musician needs to practice scales, an actor needs to practice in front of a camera on a regular basis. That camera will be the bane of your existence in auditions and on sets unless you can be completely comfortable and reveal your true emotional life in front of it. V-log, practice scenes from material you've already auditioned for, make stuff up, but tape yourself and then watch it back with a keen eye and compassionate heart. If you can't stand to watch yourself on camera, all the more reason to do it. You want *us* to watch you after all. The whole process should only take thirty minutes.

I had the good fortune to interview Sarah Drew ("Grey's Anatomy") for the second edition of my book, and she revealed during her transition from theater to film and episodic, she created a space in her tiny New York apartment in which her video camera was always setup, ready to use. She successfully taught herself to get better, with exceptional results, as you can see.

2. Do stand-up. When I teach weekly classes, I always include a unit on stand-up comedy. Unless one of my students already does stand-up or has had *some* experience with the format, most hem and haw at the prospect. They complain. One outright refused (this only happened once). I explain that getting out of your comfort zone is essential to the craft of acting. Stand-up is a very creative process. You have to zero in on who you are and write for your strengths—for your *comic persona*—that you will refine and revisit time and time again. It's also a free showcase and open mics abound all over the country. What a great way to practice performing and get exposure at the same time!

Three of my students, whom never dreamed of doing stand-up prior to the class, have gone on to perform at comedy clubs all over Southern California including at the world famous Comedy Store on Sunset Boulevard. It wasn't what they learned in class that made them successful, it was the fact that they worked on their own material regularly and grew to love the whole process.

3. Form a support group and meet weekly. Don't pursue acting in isolation; gain strength from a hand-picked community. Discuss your fears and joys honestly with each other, read scripts aloud, practice improv games, videotape one another, and watch shows online.

4. Watch network shows and YouTube videos. You must keep up with current episodic programming so you will be familiar with the style of each show should you be called in for an audition. The bread and butter of an actor's life are jobs found on network television, and now with apps and websites for all the major networks, it's easy and free to sample current episodes. Watch YouTube videos of your favorite actors and analyze why you like them so much. I can guarantee it won't be because of the way they look, but rather their ability to reveal many raw emotions in a single moment.

(Reposted from *Backstage* where I had a weekly column)

(November 2, 2014 - Los Angeles)

The Hustle

Ain't gonna like, I'm reminded every day that in order to "succeed," you have to get out of your comfort zone.

The thing you fear doing the most, you must do. An Actor, An Entrepreneur, a Leader of People—you must be comfortable on the tight rope, with the uncomfortable, otherwise, you should go do something "safe" and be happy with that.

Being an Actor, Entrepreneur, Leader is not for the faint of heart. It's for those who have *a lot* of heart—who *truly* want to make a difference, not only in their own lives or communities but out in the world at large. Those who are willing to reveal their whole soul—the dark and the light. Those who constantly *get-out-of-the-box*.

I've worked with hundreds if not thousands of actors, entrepreneurs, leaders. The hardest truth is that if you invest in yourself, you will get a return on your investment, and if you have nothing to invest (as in solvency), you are in the wrong professions.

My heart goes out to the actors especially. You all have special issues. First off, actors are required at every turn to invest in themselves— headshots, reels, classes, workshops, clothes, time, networking, creating content… well, the list is long—with absolutely no guarantee of a profit. You might make money, but to actually clear a profit? In fact, you might never make a profit, no matter how talented or determined you are.

Secondly, actors have to audition constantly and be okay (as in *not* frustrated or demoralized) if they only book a network, streaming, or cable gig twice a year, maybe less. Non-actors, can you even imagine going on 4-5 job interviews a week for a year and *never* getting a job? You would be demoralized and stop believing in yourself. Well, actors—WHO GIVE SO MUCH TO THE WORLD—live with this their whole careers no matter how "successful" they are.

"What am I doing wrong?" "How can I get to the next level?" "Why did so-and-so get that role and not me?" I hear these statements constantly. It's negative chatter and that needs to stop, otherwise, you will get so frustrated, you will become a miserable, sour person who annoys everyone around you.

(Take me as an example. I'm a very strong casting director with 24 years under my belt who now works alongside the doyenne of casting in the southeast, Shay Griffin, but there is such a stronghold in this region by one casting company that gets nearly everything in this booming market, we are without a casting job and have been for months. Do I complain and wallow in my own self-pity? Well, maybe for a few minutes . . but then I reinvent myself and my workshop/class offerings with all the many talents I have. I'm thriving in my new endeavors, and frankly, feel more authentic in what I do and how I touch people's lives.)

The fact that you are *getting* opportunities is the win. Believe me, we only ask actors to audition if we think they are really good. There are no pity auditions. There might be "let's try him or her out" auditions, but only because we saw something in their materials that sparked our interest.

Entrepreneurs and Leaders in Business, you have it so much easier, but still, it's a hustle that never lets up. What is not easy for you is to find your best, most authentic self and then share that with everyone you meet. What's more, networking is not enough, now you have to create videos of yourself talking about what you do and blast that all over social media, on your website, and on LinkedIn (which I still don't love :). Talk about "putting yourself out there"! For the non-actor to feel comfortable in front of the camera? Heaven help you. But get out-of-your-box, because that's where the rewards and "successes" truly happen.

(July 30th, 2018—Atlanta)

185

The Unsung Heroes

Recently, a good friend of mine, who is a manager, pointed out to me that in my many blog entries I never ever mention the integral role that management plays in the casting process. I immediately felt ashamed because he's so right. I often moan that casting directors don't get enough respect in the Industry for all the hard work that we do, but that's even more true for the tireless agents and managers, who are basically salesmen. And as we all know, *sales* is probably the toughest job there is. Actors, you think it's tough to get auditions? Well, it's nothing compared to what the agents and managers experience every day in volume.

Agents and Managers, in any city, are the folks in the trenches, encouraging actors every step of the way to get their shit together and keep it that way. Agents/managers advise their clients on classes, headshots, style and wardrobe. They stand up for them, coach them, loan them money, and as my friend pointed out to me "support them even when they have blown the opportunity that we spent weeks fighting to get them in the audition room."

The relationship between a casting director and an agent/manager is a symbiotic one. And even thought I often boast that I alone "discovered" this actor or that actress in a play or at The Groundlings, I *could not do my job* without the hundreds of agents and managers whom I also call friends. The closest contact a cd has in the course of a typical work day is not just with the actors auditioning but with the agents and managers. We seldom talk to other casting directors and our contact with the producers/writers/directors is very limited because they are doing their real jobs which is creating content. It's the cds and the agents/managers, in constant contact, day in and day out, helping each other do our jobs, which is to populate all the episodic shows, films, web series, plays that we love so much.

It was easy to get agents/managers on board when I was working in network episodic and the pay scale was relatively high, but I have to admit, their generosity in helping me cast projects that pay crap is humbling. I've cast several web series (*Miss Mustard Glade, Jeff and Ravi Fail History, The British* Invasion to name only a few) The agents/managers I worked with spent literally hours/days, via phone and electronically, helping me to assemble just the right cast and if one of their actors happened to book the job, they probably made $47.

Actors, stop complaining about not booking enough jobs, or worse, blaming your agent for it. It's "tough" for *everyone* in the Industry. But we do it because we love it. So go out there and be in a play or create your own content or be in an improv show. But keep an optimistic, enthusiastic outlook, and you'll be fine.

(July 16, 2017—Atlanta)

Make Us Feel Something

I had the honor to be asked by the SAGFoundation to participate in a two day summit for actors in Atlanta this weekend, and I lead a mock audition workshop with a group of sweet, vibrant people. It was a lot of fun and also informative, from both sides. The entire event was free to the actors.

I was reminded of a precept I hold dear which basically is - *Don't intellectualize the material, emotionalize it.*

As an actor, the only thing you can play is emotions. It's the only thing the audience responds to, really. You think we're attracted to hot bodies? No. We're attracted to a strong emotional inner life. Adele has won a gaggle of Grammys writing and singing songs that are extremely emotional. Apparently, whether we listen to very happy songs or very sad songs, dopamine is released when we feel and either way we are elated by this. Feeling makes us feel better.

I often ask actors "what are you feeling at the top of the scene?" Not *what do you want* or *what is your action.* A good audition, whether it be for a lead or a co-star, *especially* if it's for a co-star as there is usually very little to go on, has at least five emotional qualities. Both dark and light,

A charismatic person is the perfect balance of the two. If you are all dark qualities, you will scare us, and if you are all light qualities, we won't be emotionally moved by you. Shakespeare's plays are all about self-knowledge and balance. If you're too much of one thing, you either end up dead or your family is destroyed (Macbeth, King Lear). If you're the perfect balance of man and woman, dark and light, you end up happily married (Rosalind in As You Like It).

Once you have your five qualities and are feeling them, all simultaneously, just as we do in real life/real behavior, start the scene. Don't *think* about it too much. Absolutely don't think "I'm going to be sad on this line and optimistic on the next one." Don't map it out. Just feel it all and *go.*

Oh, and be well-prepped with the dialogue. If you are struggling with the lines, no amount of emotions can save you. You will be stuck in your head and that's doom for an audition.

(June 3, 2018—Atlanta)

Practice Acting Every Day

Auditioning for network and cable episodic shows and feature films is not the practice of acting, it's more like the final exam. If you "pass," then you will get a callback. If you practice every day and do the work and prepare with all your heart and soul, then you will more likely get a callback and hopefully book a job. But you cannot book a job without putting in your time with the boring stuff. It's kind of like a musician practicing his scales. Tedious, yes, but simply must be done, no question. If your only opportunity to act is prepping and doing an audition, then your head is not in the right place.

So how can actors practice every day? If you're not in rehearsals for a play, performing in a show, or booked on a episodic show or film, what is an actor to do? Here are some ideas, gathered with the help of my Audition Class students...

1) always be enrolled in a class of some sort—acting, improv, voice, movement, etc.

2) go over old scenes from classes and try to improve on how you did them the first time

3) write your own monologues and work on them

4) find a monologue from a full-length play and work on that

5) video tape yourself doing a monologue

6) create an actor support group and read scenes and plays together—video tape the scenes

7) make a vlog

Watch episodic shows, Netflix, and at least one film in a movie theater a week.

And if you can make money at what you practice every day, well, then you are truly blessed.

(April 30, 2017—Atlanta)

Times Change... and Dreams Do, Too

When I was an undergrad at UCLA in the dawning of the '80s, I dreamed of being a stage manager at either Oregon Shakespeare Festival in Ashland or at The Guthrie Theater in Minneapolis. I remember Michael McLain, my directing mentor, showed us photos of the stage created by Tyrone Guthrie. It was a thrust stage that connected deeply and literally into the audience, and the house was set up such that every seat was a good one, even at the top row. The Guthrie was one of the early Regional theaters in the U.S., which had a resident acting company that would perform the classics in rotating repertory with the highest professional standards and without the stresses of the commercial theater on Broadway.

I never achieved my dream of working there as a stage manager, but as a casting director I have been invited to meet with their graduating BFA students off and on since that program started in 2004, and it's usually the highlight of my year. The Guthrie's program is in conjunction with the University of Minnesota and its chief leader is Ken Washington, who personally scouts the best high school performers in the country. When these students graduate, they can do most anything—Shakespeare, the Classics, contemporary, experimental, and original plays. They all have talent, integrity, and a great work ethic. They respect the work and all those who've come before them. They always give me hope for the future of the Performing arts which never gets the attention or funding that sports programs do.

Now, as the Regional theater system as I knew and admired it 30-40 years ago is shifting and resident companies are dismantling, I wonder what to tell students who want to make a living solely in theater because they just love it so much, just as I did when I graduated college. I must tell them the truth—that the only way to make a living as an actor for the long-term is to combine theater acting with episodic, film, commercials, web series, etc. But my heart breaks a little at this because I know that the purity and joy of performing live on a formidable stage can not be replicated in front of a camera, no matter how well the episodic show or film is written.

I also know that when you graduate from college with one thing in mind, a lot can change in the ensuing years. Life takes you down roads you never imagined, as it did for me when I went into Casting. Yeah, I wanted to call a show at the Guthrie, but now that I can meet with their young actors and (hopefully) guide them through tricky territory, I'm elated and grateful.

UPDATE: Morning of April 27

Last night I had the privilege of attending the final showcase of scenes and the graduation for these very special artists. I've seen a lot of showcases in many cities and for many university theater programs in my 20 years in the casting trenches, and this one was THE best. First, each actor only did one scene. There was none of the usual "two contrasting scenes, one Shakespeare or classical, one contemporary." The night before, the actors performed in two one acts that were created specifically *for* them by playwrights that the Guthrie commissions. The program has been doing this since it's inception and it's a brilliant idea that works in spades. I don't know why all universities don't do this. The showcase of scenes I witnessed last night (which is in *addition* to the one-acts) were all perfectly chosen and cast, and they were *longer* than the usual 2 minutes. There was not this rushing on and off the stage to make way for the next couple, and no one dressed in black slacks or bright single-colored dresses. These were long excerpts from plays in which something major happened which only made me want to see the whole piece with these tremendous actors all the more. There was a good variety of playwrights represented, from Ibsen to Eulalie Spence (*Undertow*, a play I didn't know but certainly want to see in it's entirety now), Nicky Silver and Douglas Carter Beane, and of course Arthur Miller. And not a Shakespeare scene in sight, which was fine by me, but a very good rendition of *Antigone*. I've never been so emotionally moved by scenes ever.

But the extreme tears for me came at the intimate ceremony in the rehearsal hall that took place afterwards, when all the graduates gathered with their families, colleagues, teachers, support staff and future graduates. Each student gave a short speech and all thanked their parents and extended families for supporting them in their pursuit of being an actor, performer, ARTIST. Getting support from your family in a

192

profession some might think is crazy is no small feat and must be cherished like a precious and fragile gift. I certainly didn't have that when I was young…and so my tears flowed out of both deep sadness for what I missed out on and extreme pleasure for witnessing an event that gives me such hope for the future of the arts and the talent that is joining the ranks of the employed.

(April 26, 2014—Los Angeles)

(Note: Ken Washington, whom Mahershala Ali thanked in his first Oscar win, died just months after I wrote this post. He is missed by oceans of people.)

Watch Your Language

I've been staying in Baltimore, a city that I really like, but the perception of the place from those who've never been here is "The Wire," right? Why would I leave warm, beautiful Los Angeles in the dead of Winter to come to this god-forsaken place?

As an experiment, I started asking random people I've been meeting in bars (as it is NFL Playoff season after all), what is their perception of Los Angeles. All the folks I asked had never been to Los Angeles. A sampling of responses included the following: "rich people," "glamorous," "lots of parties," "traffic," "show business," "the Hollywood Hills." One cleaver man answered, "swimming pools, movie stars." When the question was asked, "what do you think of Hollywood?" every single respondent scowled or frowned in some way. Kind of like in Los Angeles when folks who've never been are asked about Baltimore. Not one person smiled and said, "I'd love to go there and live. It's a diverse, wonderful city with a lot of creative people," which is my perception of Los Angeles.

The very next week, when I was in rural Pennsylvania leading a workshop for a very talented and diverse group of theater students, I overheard the conversation to top all conversations. I was sitting at the counter of a diner, quietly eating my hearty breakfast. The older white men who were surrounding me started bad mouthing Los Angeles (and no I had not revealed where I was from)! They bandied about phrases like "oh it's a terrible place" and "Los Angeles is a Jungle." If that's not couched racism I don't know what is. What's more they were all in passionate agreement… and I said nothing. I just stewed in my French toast and felt mortified.

Hollywood or Los Angeles is like any other city. There are good people and not so good people. Most of the natives who are in their 40s and 50s are like me, children of immigrants. Quiet, well-meaning people who just wanted a chance at the American Dream. And point of fact, only 2% of the population is actually connected with the Entertainment business.

Whenever I've lead workshops, someone will inevitably make a comment about Hollywood that is couched in negative language. "I'm having trouble playing the game." "Everyone in this business is so cut-throat." "There's so much rejection." "It's who you know or what family you were born into." These kinds of comments drive me crazy and really should be eliminated from all discourse.

First off, working in the entertainment industry is not a game, it's a profession like any other. You commit to the work and put yourself out there, as you would in finance, advertising. law, or any other line of work There's rejection in any profession, but there's always opportunity for some kind of work in this field, even if acting becomes too frustrating for you. A lot of casting directors, producers, directors, and writers are ex-actors. If you love entertainment and have a real passion for it, you'll find a way to make a living.

Don't think of it as "networking," think of it as *sharing* who you are with like-minded people and connecting with them in a deep and meaningful way. Don't schmooze, just converse. Have a *conversation* with everyone you meet about what's important to you and ask others what's important to them.

Above all, avoid wrapping any topic in *negative language*. Negative language is a big turn-off. You want others attracted to you, not repelled.

There are no actual doors to knock on anymore, by the way.

And the only way to stop stereotyping is for the sensitive artists to take over the world! (If we only had the courage to speak up.)

(January 11, 2014—Baltimore, MD)

Slow Down

I recently signed up for a gym, which has these weight machines that are connected to a monitor. It helps keep you motivated as it counts out your reps, shows your range of motion, and generally keeps you on track. As I do with most everything, I hit the weights with gusto, sometimes too much gusto, prompting the monitor to flash the words "Try To Slow Down" with each movement. Sure enough, when I do follow these directions and slow way down, the exercise *is* more productive.

I often suggest to actors I coach to make a practice of sitting in a chair for at least 30 minutes and do nothing. Don't meditate. Don't listen to music. Don't journal. Don't nap. Truly *do nothing*. Unplugged. It's important for an artist (or anyone, really) to reconnect with one's self in complete quiet and calm.

Since I tell folks to do this all the time, I decided to do it myself today, after an especially busy week. *Try To Slow Down*. It's damn hard. And uncomfortable. The first 10 minutes at least are spent thinking about all the things I should be doing (watch that video an actor just sent me, respond to that email from a dear friend, clean the floors, write a blog about sitting in a chair) or realizing my lips are chapped and my feet prone to callouses are doing better. The next 5 minutes I am reminded of why I stay so 'busy' in the first place—so I don't have to obsess over all the stupid things I regret saying or doing over the course of my whole life. But then, if I wait long enough, and don't get up to retrieve my chap stick, my racing mind slows way down and I'm suddenly overcome with—what shall I call it?—a *peace* that feels like *nothing*... and it's wonderful. The daydreams can now begin.

I need to take my own advice more often. How can I be an example to others if I don't practice what I preach? Trying To Slow Down doesn't mean I'm lazy and I should not feel guilty (which I do sometimes) for taking a break, it means I can be more productive.

I hope moving forward I will sit in a chair for 30 minutes as much as I go to the gym.

(November 3rd, 2016—Atlanta)

DUTIES OF A CASTING DIRECTOR

- Negotiate CD deal
- Create deal memo and send W-9 paperwork
- Read the script
- Aid in deciding when auditions will take place
- Accumulate all info for breakdown
- Book casting space
- Create the breakdown
- Aid in deciding sides for auditions
- Post the breakdown on BS, AA, *Backstage*
- Make lists of actors I know to bring in
- Monitor the submissions from bs, aa, backstage
- Monitor and answer emails and phone calls
- Go through submissions and choose the best for the job
- Watch demo reels
- Decide who will come in
- Organize the sessions
- Call out the appointments
- Make sure each auditioner has material and directions to session
- Revise the appointments as schedules change (for the actors and producer/director)
- Create the session sheets
- Confirm all actors called in
- Revise the session sheets as actors pass or "fall out"
- Confer with director/producer re: casting ideas
- Forward demo reels to director/producer of those actors na for auditions
- Arrive early and set up first casting session (includes camera, tripod, monitor etc.)
- Run first casting session (pair up actors, bring in order of sign in, etc.)
- Tape all auditions if required
- Read with actors if necessary
- When session is complete, confer with producer/director top picks
- Decide to have additional session or just callbacks
- Dismantle the casting studio/room
- Inform top picks of their status

- Return emails and phone calls related to the session
- Convert video footage from camera to imovie
- Edit video footage (just top picks or everyone?)
- Upload video footage to website (private YouTube? Cast-It?)
- Share link with producer/director
- Prep second casting session if applicable
- Repeat all tasks related to casting session if applicable for second
- Prepare callback session
- Create callback session sheet
- Confirm casting studio for callbacks
- Confirm actors for callback session
- Reconfirm with all top picks on availability of dates of job
- Provide callback material to all top picks
- Send full script to top picks if required
- Revise callback session sheet as changes occur
- Arrive early to callback session to set up (includes camera, tripod, monitor, etc.)
- Run callback casting session (pair up actors, bring in order of sign in, etc.)
- Tape all auditions if required
- Read with actors if necessary
- When session is complete, confer with producer/director bookings
- Dismantle the casting studio/room
- Put actors on hold
- Return emails and phone calls related to the session
- Convert video footage from camera to imovie
- Edit video footage (just bookings or everyone?)
- Upload video footage to website (private YouTube? Cast-It?)
- Share link with producer/director and client if applicable
- Wait for client approval, if applicable
- Once final approvals arrive, offer each actor respective roles (if client does not approve of all the actors chosen, start process over for roles not yet cast.)
- Negotiate with agents/managers if actor has representation
- Liaison between agents/managers and producer/client
- Close all deals
- Create deal memos for all talent
- Complete deal memos for all talent (must include actor personal info)

- Make sure all talent and/or agents/managers sign the deal memos
- Forward completed deal memos to agents/managers and production
- Clear actors with SAG-AFTRA if applicable
- Create cast list if required
- Contract admin if required
- (provide feedback if time)
- Remove uploaded videos from website
- Invoice job
- Monitor payment of job
- If job not paid within 30 days, contact producer
- Additional tasks if applicable
- Hire understudies
- Hire replacements if an actor has an undisclosed conflict or is fired while on the job

(if we are also including self-tape auditions, we need to watch those, too. Or replace the in person auditions with self-tapes entirely, which is becoming more the norm. Personally, I prefer doing in person auditions.)

ACKNOWLEDGEMENTS

Beaty Reynolds, my writing mentor and exquisite friend. Thank you for encouraging me to write the first edition in 2009 in the first place and going over the first draft with me sentence by sentence.

Jeff Greenberg, who was the casting director on *Frasier* for its eleven-year run. He gave me my big break into casting, and we worked side by side as his associate for eight of those years. He changed my life. There would be no book if it were not for him and all he taught and shared with me.

Julie Haber, for being a generous friend for years and introducing me to Jeff.

Marc Hirschfeld, for hiring me as Manager of Casting at NBC and being a great person with exquisite taste in actors.

All the **agents** in Los Angeles, New York, and Atlanta. You are the unsung heroes.

All the **actors**, of course. Can't make movies, episodic, and theatre without you!

Cris Gross, the best, most steadfast friend I have had—at 36 years and counting. The first and second editions couldn't have been published without you.

Adam LeBow, who painstakingly edited this third edition. He brings so much knowledge and insight to any community he's a part of. Glad he's been a part of mine in two different cities.

Made in United States
Orlando, FL
27 August 2022

21631710R00124